Dear Amir Jinnah,
    Join me on a journey into our past
through the pages of this book. Thank
you for your interest.
                    Warm regards,
                    Ameer Janmohamed.
                        12/11/08

Ameer Janmohamed
104/25 Brewhouse Lane
London SW15 2JX
akj85@btinternet.com

To my parents

My father
Kassam Janmohamed
(1905-1950)
&
My mother
Rabhia Janmohamed
(1910-1999)

A
REGAL ROMANCE
and other memories

AMEER JANMOHAMED

www.societybooks.com

First published in Great Britain in 2008 by

Society Books
Books & Life Limited
17-21 Wyfold Road
London, SW6 6SE
United Kingdom
www. societybooks.com

A catalogue record for this book is available from the British Library

ISBN 978-0-9558131-0-8 Hardback

Cover and layout design: Lily Mebratu

Society Books practices policies of using papers that are natural, renewable and recyclable products
and made from wood grown in sustainable forests. The logging and manufacturing processes are expected
to conform to environmental regulations of the country of origin.

Printed and bound in England by Biddles Limited, King's Lynn, Norfolk.

CONTENTS

Acknowledgements

There are so many people without whose help this book could never have been written. May I say thank you to at least some of them. I would like to thank the following for providing me with inspiration, guidance and benefit of their not inconsiderable experience and expertise, and for having laboriously checked some of my earlier drafts, and for their invaluable criticisms, gratefully taken on board:

Cynthia Salvadori
Shariffa Keshavjee
Azmeena Ladha

I would like to gratefully acknowledge the writings and research of the following individuals, which have proved extremely helpful to me in the writing of this book:

Edward Rodwell	Olive Hallam
Hassanali HS Verjee	Sultanali Valli-Hasham
Mumtaz Ali TajddinSadik Ali	Nuruddeen Somji
Kassamali Paroo	Shamash Verjee

I would also like to thank the following individuals for their direct contributions, which have been incorporated within different chapters.

Yusuf Keshavjee	Taj Dhala
Sadiq Ghalia	Kass Verjee

SPECIAL THANKS: The period between 1968 and 1971 was easily the busiest period of my life. I was simultaneously the President of the Aga Khan Council Mombasa, Governor of Rotary International District 220, Director of a number of companies including the Diamond Jubilee Investment Trust Ltd, and was actively involved in the running of Badrudin's Sports House, and partner in Regal Cinema in Mombasa. All this would not have been possible were it not for the help and support of my mother, my sisters and Zeenat, and three individuals whom I would particularly like to mention below.

ZAHER HUSSEIN SULEMAN DAMJI, affectionately known to all as Zaher Mama. Zaher Mama smilingly and uncomplainingly managed Badrudin's Sports House during that busy period, and indeed a few preceding years whilst I was involved in the Ismaili Jamat as the Kamadia and then the Mukhi of the Kuze Jamat Khana in Mombasa.

MOHAMED ABDULLAH as the Hon. Secretary, and LUTUF MAHERALI as the Member for Economics in the Aga Khan Council Mombasa, who chaired the Council meetings when I was away. Thanks to both of them for covering for me during my frequent and often prolonged absences from Mombasa on Rotary business. We clearly had a happy

Council as seen in this photo taken when we visited the Mayor's Parlour in 1969.

Left to right: Amin Dhala, Sadru Nurmohamed Adam, Lutuf
Maherali, Jimmy Nasser Alibhai, Mohamed Abdullah, Zul Allibhai,
His Worship the Mayor and myself signing the Visitor's Book.

My very special thanks to my right-hand man, our grandson IMRAN JANMOHAMED, who patiently helped me with the production of this book, taught me how to get the best out of my computer, and who has rescued me several times when I have managed to entangle myself in the intricacies of various computer programmes. To that I would add my thanks to our son QUASSIM and our daughter-in-law NAZIRA for allowing Imran to leave the family home in Toronto and come and work with me in London, which also happens to be his birthplace. He was born in St. Teresa's Hospital in Wimbledon in 1982.

This book bears the unmistakable imprint of three individuals who must be mentioned. Foremost is my publisher, HOM PARIBAG of Society Books, who envisioned this book in its present form. I thank him for the confidence he has shown in my writing.

Next is my copy editor, MARGARET LAIRD, who brought order where there was chaos. She organised my writing into paragraphs and chapters and tried to instill in me some sense of linguistic discipline.

Last but by no means the least, LILY MEBRATU, who with Hom Paribag is responsible for the excellent design and layout of the book, made especially difficult due to the number of pictures and captions. My sincere thanks to all three.

Thanks also to HUGH HILL for an excellent potrait of a reluctant subject.

AUTHOR'S NOTE

I sometimes wonder if in a previous incarnation, I might have been an archivist, or a librarian, a diarist or perhaps even a filing clerk. For I have always had this compulsion to record, collect, collate, and organise information, data, photos, newspaper cuttings, books, and the like. And to keep diaries – and more diaries. And then index and arrange them in a manner where retrieval of data is possible.

Having had a long and full life, this penchant has resulted in a collection of photos, diaries, notes, and memorabilia etc.,which allows me to take a peek into my past whenever I want to. I am hugely grateful to my mother Rabhia and my sisters Roshan and Sultan for having saved and preserved priceless family photos and documents, which form the basis of my archives, and without which I would not have been able to access memories which lurk in the recesses of my mind.

I cannot thank Zeenat enough for having salvaged so many of my personal papers, albums, diaries and books and especially for having brought them to London, after my departure from Kenya in December 1972.

As is the way of the elderly, I frequently bore people ad nauseam with stories and anecdotes about how things used to be in the past. Listeners have at times urged me to commit my memories to paper. They (out of kindness, no doubt) said that the information I had in my head would otherwise be lost to posterity when I died. In reality they might have felt that I would stop boring them with my stories once I started writing them down! So, this is my attempt to humour them. I suppose it might also in some small measure be a chronicle, or a snapshot, of the times through which we lived in Kenya in the nineteen-twenties, thirties and forties, as seen through the eyes of a young middle class Indian boy born with a 'plated' silver spoon in his mouth.

As Mike Owuor of the Nairobi Standard writes in his review of Shariffa Keshavjee's book Bwana Mzuri, "Some hold the belief that family histories are best handed down orally. However, failing to record such information makes it permeable to distortion". So - I have written about events and people as I remember them. This is my personal take on events, and things I have learnt from various sources, hearsay quite often, verbally and in print. Obviously, therefore, everything is filtered through the lenses of my own eyes and tinted with my subjective perception of events and people. I realise that there are not too many people of my generation around who shared my life and times. So I do not have the luxury of consulting with my contemporaries, let alone finding corroboration of my recollections. Inevitably therefore, this is a very personal account of people and events. I believe that people are what they are because of their pasts. I am a product of my parents, and their parents, and their ancestors, and I am what I am because of what they were, where they were, and what happened to them. I felt that I could give my past some perspective by simultaneously looking at other events which were happening in the past, elsewhere in the world, but had some bearing on my life, no matter how vicariously or remotely. This has led me to prepare a somewhat ambitious Chronology of Events (which appears at the end of the book). This chronology juxtaposes events which occurred in other parts of the world, but more or less in the same time frame.

This Chronology is personal and, to some extent, arbitrary, and yet with some imagination, I perceive all listed events as having had some bearing on the lives of my ancestors, no matter how vicariously, and thus also on me and who I am. I choose to describe myself as a Kenya born, British Ismaili Muslim of Indian origin, whose home (and heart) is in London, and with a Gandhian abhorrence of violence. This makes me susceptible to emotional turmoil occasionally, especially when I am watching World Cup Cricket! On the other hand, I believe it gives me immunity from jingoism.

My forefathers were Hindu Lohanas and probably converted to the Ismaili Muslim faith in the fourteenth century, perhaps even later. This would have been the time when Ismaili Pirs came to India from Persia, with a view to propagate the faith. They refer to India as Jampoo Dip in our Ginans. This also means that if I wanted to explore the history of my family, going back several hundred years, I would have to take into account the fact that my forebears embraced the Ismaili Muslim faith in (approximately) the time of the 30th Imam, Imam Islam Shah, and prior to that they were Hindus. Thus ancient Hindu history also has relevance for me in this context.

For me, life has been like a colourful tapestry, with many different coloured strands running through it. I have lived. I have loved. And I have been loved. Beautiful memories – and, of course, sad and poignant ones too - are etched on my soul. I acknowledge that life has dealt me a better than fair hand. Therefore, whenever I pray gratitude is on a par with supplication. Inevitably, as I try to recount my memories, I pick up a thread here and then jump to another one there, but they are all interwoven - before returning to the original thread. The result may be a little disjointed, but that is to be expected as one meanders through one's memories. I lack the presumption to call this book my "memoirs" – rather, I am just revisiting here all those people, places and events which are important to me, and which have coloured and enhanced the tapestry of my life, especially in my earlier years. I have taken the opportunity of including some photos that illustrate some interesting moments and people in my life.

This book is not about my present, nor my recent past. It is mainly about events which happened in the last century and before – in the previous millennium, as a matter of fact. It is also mostly about people who have "Passed on to Higher Service", as they might say in Rotary!

Ameer Janmohamed.

xiii

FAMILY HISTORY

FAMILY TREE DIAGRAM
(Male Members)

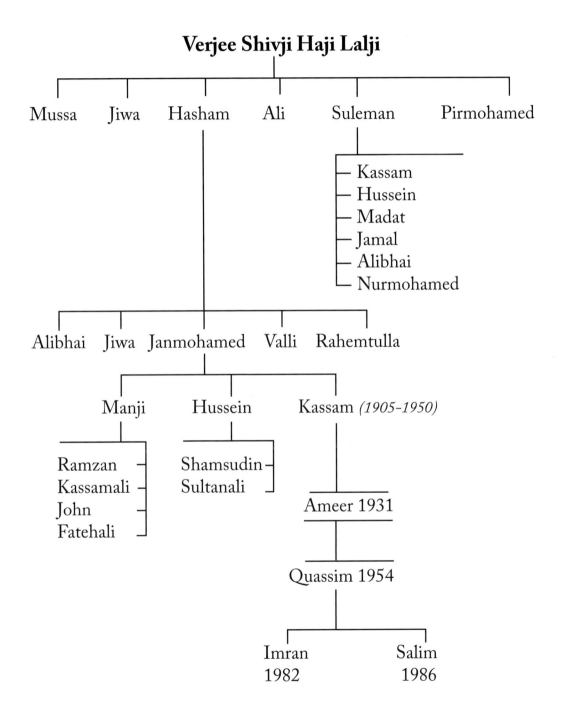

Verjee Shivji Haji Lalji

Mussa Jiwa Hasham Ali Suleman Pirmohamed

— Kassam
— Hussein
— Madat
— Jamal
— Alibhai
— Nurmohamed

Alibhai Jiwa Janmohamed Valli Rahemtulla

Manji Hussein Kassam *(1905-1950)*

Ramzan
Kassamali
John
Fatehali

Shamsudin
Sultanali

Ameer 1931

Quassim 1954

Imran
1982

Salim
1986

My Forefathers

According to my late uncle Sultanali Valli-Hasham, my full name, going back several generations, is Ameerally Kassam Janmohamed Hasham Verjee Shivji Haji Kajia. This reflects our society's custom whereby people usually call themselves by their first name, followed by their father's name and then the grandfather's name - and so on.

I came across a reference to my great, great, great, grandfather Shivji Haji in Hassanali Hussein Suleman Verjee's diary "The Verjee Family: Pioneers in East Africa – 1800-1992". Hassanali Kaka writes as follows:

"The history of my (Verjee) family, businessmen, adventurers and community leaders, really begins in India with my great grandfather Shivji Haji. Shivji, the oldest son of Haji, lived in the town of Kajmason in Kathiawar, in the province of Gujarat and gained renown for a spectacular act of bravery.

He was working as an administrative officer in the town one day in 1800, when a gang of thugs raided the area, looting and killing many innocent people. Shivji was an educated, highly intelligent man who combined a keen sense of responsibility with courage, and he fought off the mob single-handed and drove them away.

The news of this feat reached the Raja of the province, who showed his appreciation and respect by visiting the town and calling a mass meeting at which he commended the local hero. He presented Shivji with a gift in the form of a monthly collection of the province's revenue for his personal use for the duration of his life. Shivji collected this revenue for a number of years as decreed, but eventually the province was hit by a series of disastrous draughts and the revenue became insufficient to support his large family.

Reluctantly, he resolved to forego the Raja's gift and moved with his wife and children, the oldest being Verjee, to Una where he amassed a considerable fortune. Before his death he donated one double-storey building valued at 150,000 rupees to the Ismailia community (Jamat) and another, worth 200,000 rupees to the town of Una for use as a hostel."

Verjee had six sons. They were Mussa, Hasham, Suleman, Jiwa, Ali and Pirmohamed. Sadly, I have no information on Mussa, Jiwa, Ali and Pirmohamed Verjee. However, descendants of Suleman Verjee went on to distinguish themselves in Africa in trade, commerce, politics and education. I have no doubt that a definitive history of the Suleman Verjee family would make fascinating reading. (Suleman Verjee grand-sons are also mentioned in the chapter "The Brynmelyn Boys" in this book as well, since a number of them were with my father at Brynmelyn College in Weston-Super-Mare in the nineteen-twenties.) *See note 1 on page 21.*

HASHAM VERJEE
MY GREAT GRANDFATHER

Hasham Verjee had five sons named Alibhai, Jiwa, Valli, Janmohamed and Rahemtullah. I have been fortunate enough to have met descendants of Alibhai and Jiwa Hasham. Rahemtullah had no issue. I have met Jaffer (Motabapa) Alibhai and his son Kassamali who used to own Alibhai's Service Station in Kampala. And I met Hassan Kaka, son of Jiwa Hasham. He was married to Gulbanu, daughter of Habib Motan. They lived in Nairobi. I remember him as a handsome, sporting type, with a rich crop of Brilliantined black hair.

JANMOHAMED HASHAM VERJEE
MY GRANDFATHER

In a legal document dated November 1927, my grandfather describes himself as "I, Janmohamed Hasham Verjee of Mombasa in the Kenya Protectorate and originally from Gadhra in the State of Junagadh, India". He had seven children: three sons, Manji, Hussein and my father Kassam; and four daughters, Bhani, Jena, Sikina and Fatma. My uncles Manji Motabapa and Hussein Motabapa were born in Gadhra. My father Kassam was born in Mombasa. I assume that my aunts Bhani Fai and Jena Fai would have been born in India, and Sikina Fai and Fatma Fai in Kenya.

In the matter of names, it is my observation that Ismaili men with names ending in "ji" or "'jee", such as Manji, Keshavjee, Shivji, Walji, Verjee, Hirji, Kanji, Velji, Somji etc. were more than likely to have been born in India. Ismaili boys born in India were given these names to make it easier for them to be assimilated in the predominantly Hindu environment in which they dwelt.

These names appear to have gone out of fashion with the East African Ismailis. Boys born in Africa were more likely to be named Kassam, Hussein, Hasham, Sultan, Rahemtullah, Madatally, and so on. The name Amir, or Ameer, was very much in fashion in Kisumu in Kenya in the early 1930s. I can think of several. There was Amir Hasham Jamal, Amir Ishani, Amir Rahemtullah Kassam Lakha, Amir Madhavjee, Amir Ebrahim Kassam, and myself, all born within a year or so of each other in Kisumu.

.

COMING TO AFRICA

I cannot establish with any degree of certainty exactly when my grandfather Janmohamed Hasham came to Africa. Various snippets of information seem to suggest that my grandparents, known to me as Dadabapa and Dadima, came to Mombasa circa 1895. My uncle Manji Janmohamed joined the family in 1905, which was the year my father Kassam was born in Mombasa.

In those days the only way in which people could sail from one place to another was by means of Dhows. Dhows from Kathiawar and Kutch in India mainly set sail from the ports of Mandvi or Porbandar or Diu on the north-western coast of India. They usually hugged the coast-line and made calls to ports like Gwadar in Baluchistan, and Muscat in Oman, before sailing southwards along the African Coast-line. They might stop over in Mogadishu in Somalia. Further south lay their destination ports in Kenya, Tanganyika and Portuguese East Africa.

I was told the following story, which if true, is simply fascinating and quite romantic. I have been told that when my grandfather left India in 1895 to seek his fortune, his destination was actually Portuguese East Africa, now known as Mozambique, rather than British East Africa. Apparently the voyage from India had been quite rough, and my grandmother in particular had suffered not only from sea-sickness but also the indignity of having to perform her ablutions in the unsatisfactory sanitary arrangements on the dhow.

Indian and Arab dhows had not changed significantly over a period of time. I had the opportunity to study them at close quarters when they were anchored in the Old Port in

6

Mombasa in the nineteen-forties and fifties. Their arrival was seasonal and regular. Winter Monsoons would bring sailing ships from India and Arabia to the east coast of Africa during the second half of the year. The captains of the dhows, who were called Nahodas, would have loaded their dhows with return cargo and could pick up the summer Monsoons which provided them with a fair wind for their return voyage to India in the first half of the year. (*See Note 2, Page* **22***)*

Noticeable features of these dhows were the "D" shaped wooden toilet cubicles sticking out on the sides, usually at the stern. The straight side was attached to the dhow and the rounded bit stuck out over the water. The occupant would need to squat atop a hole in the floor of the cubicle, and would need to hang on to the sides. The cubicle was open to the skies and the sides were only high enough to protect one's modesty, with the head of the occupant visible to all. Provided was a small bucket attached to a line, so that the occupant could lower the tin into the sea when water was needed.

As the story goes, when their dhow touched Mombasa for re-provisioning and essential repairs, my grandfather made the mistake of taking his long suffering wife ashore. Once she had firm ground under her feet, she simply refused to board the dhow again. My grandfather argued that their destination was Portuguese East Africa, which was still several weeks of sailing away, and that they were expected there by the friend who had actually invited him to take the trip in the first place. She would not be persuaded. She told him that he must go on and leave her behind if he really wanted to carry on. She was prepared to die where she was, but she was simply not getting on that dhow again.

According to the story, the old man had no choice but to retrieve his few belongings from the dhow, and get off at Mombasa. The rest, as they say, is history.

This story is not as improbable as it may sound at first. Portuguese East Africa had certainly attracted a number of Indian immigrants at the time. Even Suleman Verjee, who was the first member of the family to arrive in Kenya had sent two of his brothers, Nurmohamed and Jamal, to check out the possibilities in Mozambique. Although India was largely under British rule, there were a number of Portuguese enclaves, such a Goa, on the West Coast of the sub-continent, and it was

A typical Dhow

7

known that they had a colony in Africa which too offered prospects.

I sometimes speculate on what would have been the history of our family had my grandmother not put her foot down – both literally and metaphorically - in Mombasa, Kenya. I believe my grandfather would have prospered in Portuguese East Africa just as well as he did in Kenya. We would all have been born there - and I might have been a resident of Lisbon rather than London today - and this book might well have been written in Portuguese rather than English.

DADIMA PANBAI AND HER ALTERNATE MEDICINE

My grandmother's name was Pan. She was a very beautiful lady. She was very fair and had skin through which you could see her veins and she had limpid grey green eyes. She must have been very fit too. Unusually for those days she had given birth to seven children, and survived. Most men in those days were re-married, sometimes more than once, because their previous wives had died in child-birth.

Those were days of prolific families, when men were virile and wives fecund. Those were days when a man's wealth was judged by the size of his herd. Sex was more procreational than recreational. Children were not expensive because each child was supposed to bring his or her own "rozee" when they were born – they slept several to a room and education was not expensive, when it was available. And of course there was high mortality. Not many children made it to adulthood. (*See Note 3, Page 22*)

My grandmother had a long life, although it was her misfortune to witness the deaths, not only of her husband in 1931, but also of her two younger sons, Hussein in 1947 and Kassam in 1950, during her life-time.

My earliest memory of her is in our house in Mnazi Moja. My father was still in England. My mother, Roshan, Sultan and I shared the ground floor with her. We occupied two bedrooms at one end, and she occupied two rooms at the other end. The bedrooms on either side were connected by a large hall which also served as the main dining area for the family. Hussein Motabapa and his wife Sikina and their nine children occupied the first floor which had a similar layout.

9

I also remember my Dadima Panbai in another, bizarre context. I was very young and my father was still in England. Apparently I contracted what was then diagnosed as Double Pneumonia. Medicines prescribed by local doctors did not appear to work. My grandmother insisted that "alternate" medicine should be tried. Her brand of "alternate" medicine was something called "Ganga". It was a combination of incantations, voodoo, and a lot of smoke, billowing from a hand held brazier. She apparently had great faith in a lady called Manu Ma in the tailor Bazaar who was a practitioner of the cult of "Ganga". Manu Ma was brought in to see me. She said that an "evil eye" had been cast on me, and that a live sacrifice was needed to dispel its effects.

I lay on a metal frame bed, with four up-rights supporting the mosquito net, which formed a square tent around me. In a gruesome ceremony, a live chicken was brought inside my mosquito net. Manu Ma, with my grandmother at her side, recited mantras, while our house-boy was ordered to cut the poor bird's throat. I ended up with a lot of blood on me, as did the mosquito net. I was told this story when I was a little older. I used to wake up in a cold sweat when I visualised the scene, with a squawking chicken desperately flapping its wings, its throat slit, a few inches from my head, amid a spray of blood and flying feathers.

The "Ganga" did not work. In desperation Hussein Motabapa then decided to get a European doctor from Nairobi, a Dr. Endser, to visit me. He asked the family why I was lying in a darkened room with no fresh air. He demanded that all the wooden slatted windows be flung open. He said I should be taken regularly to the beach and put into salt water. That is when our family started going to the Thiwi Beach on the South Coast. And he prescribed two tonics. One was foul-tasting Scott's Cod Liver Oil - you had to swallow two tablespoons, for capsules had not yet been thought of - and the other was a stuff called Waterbury's Compound, which was quite addictive. Over a period of time I must have consumed both by the gallon. I know that my family used to order them by the case.

Although I survived, I have been left with this legacy of respiratory problems, which I am afraid Quassim and Imran and Salim will have to watch out for.

VALLI HASHAM AND COMPANY

The picture on next page shows the European in the middle wearing a pith helmet. It was the common headgear for Europeans in the tropics, to protect them from sunstrokes. Coloured people were supposed to be immune. The pith hemlet was also referred to as a sun helmet, or a topee. The Gujarati word for a hat is topee. Hence people who wore a topee were quiet often referred to as to 'topiaras'. In fact Indians talking among themselves would regularly refer to Europians as 'topiaras' In the picture above it is interesting to note that both my father Kassam Janmohamed and my uncle Manji Janmohamed are also wearing topees. My father must have been on a visit from London, for at that time he was a student there.

It is also interesting to note that all of them have heads covered. My grandfather Janmohamed Hasham and his brother Valli Hasham are wearing the traditional long coats which Khoja businessmen of the time used to wear. My father and his two brothers are wearing European style suits, but Husssein Motabapa is wearing the traditonal Khoja cap, which unlike the pith helmet did not provide much protection from the glare of the sun.

My grandfather Janmohamed Hasham and his brother Valli Hasham were in business together since their early days in Kenya and traded under the name of Valli Hasham & Company. I have a page from an unidentified early publication which lists prominent businesses in Eastern Africa and Rhodesia, and this is how they describe Valli Hasham and Co. General Merchants and Commission Agents, PO Box 121, Mombasa:

"If a stranger to Mombasa starts out to discover the premises of Messrs. Valli Hasham and Co., the search may be somewhat difficult, but very interesting; and when at last the firm's offices are reached they will be found in one of the quaintest parts of old Mombasa, tucked away in a back street, in front

11

of a parapeted well about which many stories could undoubtedly be told. Messrs Valli Hasham and Co. require no advertising, for they are one of the best-known and largest Indian firms in the town, and transact a considerable share of local trade, especially in blankets, piece-goods, wire-netting, building materials, etc.

Their name is also well known and esteemed in manufacturing circles in Europe, America, and elsewhere, and is a synonym for commercial honour and financial security in everything with which they have been connected.

The partners are two brothers, Messrs. Valli Hasham and Janmohamed, whose rise to fortune and fame forms one of the romances of local trade. About thirty-two years ago they started in a

1928/1929 Photo, taken in Kisumu, shows from left to right: Kassam Janmohamed, Janmohamed Hasham, unidentified European, Valli Hasham, Hussein Janmohamed and Manji Janmohamed.

very small way, and little was it realised then that their undertaking was destined in time to become one of the most successful and influential mercantile concerns in East Africa. The firm have branches at Nairobi and Kisumu, and own very much property there as well as in Mombasa."

Both brothers believed in brick and mortar and owned numerous properties in various towns in Kenya. The Regal Cinema in Mombasa was perhaps their most ambitious project. I have written the story of the Regal elsewhere in this book, and is indeed the inspiration for this book. This desire to invest in brick and mortar has been handed down from one generation to another and continues to this date.

MY GRANDFATHER'S DEATH

A s mentioned earlier, 1931 was an eventful year for the family. The construction of the Regal Cinema was completed. I was born in Kisumu, 500 miles inland on the shores of Lake Victoria on 6th June 1931. And my grandfather died only 12 days later, on 18th June, in Mombasa.

The news of my birth had been conveyed to him as he lay on his death-bed in Mombasa. He refused to believe that Kassam's wife had given birth to a son. He said, "You are trying to make a dying man happy by saying that Kassam's wife has delivered a boy." His scepticism was based on the fact that my mother had delivered three daughters in a row so far.

His oldest son Manji already had two sons, Ramzan and Kassamali, and two daughters, Rehmat and Shirin. (John and Fatehali were born later). And Husssein Motabapa's wife had also produced two sons, Shamsu and Sultanali, and five daughters, Dolu, Gulbanu, Shirin, Malek and Noor. (Munira and Gulzar came later). It had been a matter of regret for him that my father did not have a male heir. He almost certainly passed away not believing that I had been born.

I sometimes wish there was some way in which he could have known about me. He might have been pleased with me for having succeeded in following in his footsteps in one particular aspect. He served as the Mukhi of Mombasa Kuze Jamat Khana 1925-1927. His Kamadia was Maherali Valli Issa. Thirty-nine years later I had the same privilege. My Kamadia was Aziz Kassim-Lakha. (Before that, I had served as the Kamadia, with Mohamedali Rashid as my Mukhi – a good man, who taught me so much about Jamati customs, religious practices, and how a Kamadia ought to deport himself, with decorum, dignity and gravitas.)

My grandfather served as the President of Aga Khan Ismaili Provincial Council for Mombasa 1928-1931, and I was privileged to do the same exactly forty years later. His oldest son Manji had also served first as the President of the Kisumu Council, and then the Nairobi Provincial Council between 1930 and 1946.

His health had begun to fail some months before he died in June 1931. He made his last Will and Testament in March 1931. The Will was prepared by a Mr. AC Ross, Barrister-at-Law, Mombasa, and witnessed by Habib Abdulla, Law Clerk, Mombasa. The Will appointed his three sons Manjibhai, Husseinbhai and Kassambhai as Executors and they were directed to distribute his estate between his next of kin according to Hindu Law. He also declared that "since the coming of age of my son Kassambhai I and my said sons have been equal partners in all my property". The Will is signed Janmohamed Hasham in Gujarati.

(I believe that since Ismailis were fairly recent immigrants from India, the British administration in Kenya had decreed that the Hindu Law of Succession would be applicable to them, as distinct from the Muslim Law of Succession as derived from the Sharia, which was applied to other Muslims of non-Indian descent. I understand that this was amended in latter years. It is also my understanding that at this moment in time Ismailis follow the laws of the land in which they live, in matters of Intestacy and Succession.)

Janmohamed Hasham had arrived from India in 1895 without resources. By dint of hard work, entrepreneurship, and good fortune, he died in 1931 a wealthy man. He left behind him his share in a thriving business and properties in Kisumu, Nairobi and Mombasa. He also left behind him a name synonymous with probity and integrity.

He is buried in the Ismaili Cemetery on Makupa Road in Mombasa. His grave is situated near the Mosque within the cemetery and bears an appropriate inscription.

The Family Businesses After 1931

The firm of Valli Hasham & Company continued to trade after my grandfather's death in 1931. The following year my father decided to return to London to continue his studies. He gave his Power of Attorney to his uncle Vallibhai Hasham. This document was prepared in London by a John Alfred Donnison, of Whittington Avenue EC3, City of London, Notary Public. My father has signed the document twice; once as 'Kassam Janmohamed' and then again as "Kassim J. Verjee". The solicitor then confirmed that "The names or signatures 'Kassam Janmohamed' and 'Kassim J. Verjee' set and subscribed opposite the seal affixed at the foot of the said Power of Attorney are of the proper handwriting of the said Kassam Jan Mahomed."

This problem, of having names spelt in different ways, and being referred to with different surnames, has been a constant source of confusion for many people of Indian origin, including members of my family. I suspect there are two principal reasons for this. Firstly, the officers who issued birth certificates in English wrote the names as they heard them. These birth certificates became the basis on which Passports were issued and mistakes were thus perpetuated.

Secondly, having a family name or a surname is a fairly new thing in our society, and really became more prevalent, and useful, when our people started to settle in Western countries. People usually called themselves by their first name, followed by their father's and then the grandfather's name. For instance, my grandfather was known as Janmohamed Hasham Verjee. My father called himself Kassam Janmohamed Hasham, I used to be Ameerally Kassam Janmohamed, before I decided to opt for Janmohamed as my family name.

My mother was not entirely happy that I had dropped my father's name and preferred to be known simply as Ameer Janmohamed. Our son Quassim calls himself EQ Janmohamed, and his sons are Imran and Salim Janmohamed respectively. However, my mother continued to call herself Mrs. Kassam and was generally known as Mrs. Kassam.

The partnership of Valli Hasham & Company was dissolved in 1933. Valli Hasham died in July 1937. Sometime after that his eldest son Madatally re-established himself as Valli Hasham & Company and started trading from premises in the Indian Bazaar.

The heirs of Janmohamed Hasham and the four younger sons of Valli Hasham continued to jointly own some properties, most importantly the Regal Theatre in Mombasa.

HUSSEINI SILK STORE

Manji Janmohamed left Kisumu in 1933 and settled in Nairobi. He started a business called Husseini Silk Store, on Government Road. My father's eldest sister Bhanibai already had a flourishing business in Kisumu which was called Janmohamed Silk Store.

My father finally returned from England in January 1939. It was decided that he would make his home in Nairobi and join his brother Manji Janmohamed in the family business. Husseini Silk Store occupied a double fronted shop in a pink building on Government Road. Other prominent businesses on Government Road at the time included Kenya Fish & Provision Supplies, Mohamedali Rattansi, Alibhai Gulam, Alibhai Haji, Alibhai Shariff, and round the corner, Ahamed Brothers and Kassam Kanji, among others. All their shops were situated within a five minute walk from the Nairobi Jamat Khana, which with its clock tower, was the landmark building on Government Road.

Husseini Silk Store was Nairobi's leading haberdasher and stockist of ladies dress materials, Gor-ray pleated skirts, Pringle Twin Sets and other famous British labels, and had a number of skilled ladies tailors. The store had an upper class clientele, which included the portly figure of Lady Mitchell, wife of Sir Phillip Mitchell, the then Governor of Kenya, who had an account with Husseini Silk Store and was a frequent visitor. She always dropped in unannounced. The first that the staff would know of her coming was when the Governor's chauffeur-driven limousine would pull up outside the shop in one of the angled parking bays on Government Road, causing a small crowd of curious onlookers to gather at a respectful distance.

Lady Mitchell was particularly fond of Manji Motabapa's two sons, Ramzan and Kassamali, and it was understood that they had to drop everything and attend to her personally whenever she entered the emporium. Both of them had the gift of the gab, were excellent salesmen, and had just the right blend of respectful cheekiness which endeared them to all the upper-crust ladies who patronised Husseini Silk Store. I can still picture in my mind the flourish with which they unfurled yards and yards of the most expensive materials as they kept up a patter with the ladies.

I don't remember many, if any, Indian customers. But since the First Lady of Kenya, the Governor's wife patronised the establishment, it followed that the wives of senior officials, administrators, farmers, businessmen, Consular Corps, and all Europeans who could afford it, felt that they too had to shop there. Other prominent but occasional customers were Lady Twining and Lady Cohen, wives of the Governors of Tanganyika and Uganda.

It was a great sign of distinction for the shop that the Begum Aga Khan had dresses made there when she accompanied Sir Sultan Mohamed Shah to Nairobi. The family proudly treasures a letter from the Begum Aga Khan, praising the quality of the tailoring, about which she kindly said "…the work you did for me was most excellent and indeed I know of no house in Europe that could have done it better…"

HUSSEIN BROS

1945 picture shows Manji Janmohamed family being honoured by a visit from Sultan Mohamed Shah at their home in Sclaters Road, Nairobi. Seated from left to right: son John, my Aunt Santok, Sultan Mohamed Shah, Manji Motabapa and son Fatehali. Standing: son Kassamali, daughter-in-law Malek, her husband Ramzan and my father, Kassam Janmohamed.

There were further changes within the family in 1940. By mutual agreement, the three brothers decided to dissolve their partnership. They decided that Manji Janmohamed would retain Husseini Silk Store and the bulk of the Nairobi properties. Manji Motabapa also decided to retire that year and handed over the shop to his sons Ramzan and Kassamali.

Brothers Hussein and Kassam Janmohamed took over the business of Regal Cinema and all family properties in Mombasa, which included City House. This meant that my father, mother, two sisters and myself moved to Mombasa. World War II had now entered into its second year.

The two brothers established themselves as Hussein Brothers, and retained the PO Box no 121, Mombasa, which was the address of the original Valli Hasham & Company. Our office was in one of our own properties on Salim Road, opposite what used to be the Native Hospital and is now the main Post Office in Mombasa. The office used to be managed by Mr Odhavjee Anandjee. Odhavjee Bhai was a trusted confidante, financial controller and General Manager, all rolled into one. I don't think too much trading was done from that office. The family were focussed on properties. Over a period of years a number of plots were acquired and developed on Salim Road, Kilindini Road, Tudor, Shelly beach and Bamburi beach.

Hussein Motabapa passed away in 1947 and my father died in 1950. That was effectively the end of Hussein Bros as such, although our property partnership continued, culminating in the redevelopment of the City House in Mombasa in 1957.

Notes

Note 1 from page 3
London Jamat Mukhi/Kamadia 1936

As a matter of fact, Sultan Mohamed Shah, the 48th Imam of the Shia Imami Ismaili Community, by an appointment letter dated 10th April 1936, was graciously pleased to appoint my father, whom he refers to as Kassam Janmohamed Verjee, as the Mukhi of London Jamat, and Bahadurali Kassam Suleman Verjee as the Kamadia.

According to my mother, the Jamat consisted of between fifteen and twenty Ismaili students plus occasional Ismaili visitors from abroad. We used to live in an apartment in Earl's Court. As the Mukhi, my father would send a post card to members of the Jamat that therewould be a Jamat Khana in our apartment on such and such a day. My mother remembered that attendance by the students was very good, for they knew that the Mukhiani would provide them with a slap-up, home made Indian meal after the Jamat Khana was over. My father would also periodically take the Jamat to the Ritz Hotel in Piccadilly whenever Sultan Mohamed Shah granted them an audience.

Note 2 from page
The Jubilee Swimmimg Club

On a note of interest, I used to be a member of the Jubilee Swimming Club *(picture on page 182/183)*. The club owned a rowing boat which was moored in the Old Port which would take us each morning to the opposite shore where we swam. During the height of the dhow season, our rowing boat would have to make its way through the maze of anchored dhows from India and Arabia, with a smattering of local dhows which plied their trade between Mombasa, Malindi and Lamu along the Kenya coast. We thus had a good opportunity to study life on board.

Note 3 from page 9
Additional details of family members

Old man Verjee had six sons and a number of daughters. Suleman Verjee had six sons and two daughters. Kassam Suleman Verjee had seven sons and four daughters. Madatali Suleman Verjee had five sons and three daughters. Hussein Suleman Verjee had seven sons and four daughters.

Valli Hasham had six sons and four daughters. Janmohamed Hasham had three sons and four daughters. Manji Janmohamed had four sons and two daughters, and Hussein Janmohamed had two sons and seven daughters. My father, Kassam Janmohamed bucked the trend, for he and my mother were content with a son and three daughters, one of whom, Malek Sultan, died in her infancy. At the other end of the spectrum, Roshan, Sultan and I all ended up by having one child apiece, namely Azmeena, nano Quassim, and moto Quassim.

At the same time, my aunts too were no less prolific than their brothers. Bhani Fai, who was married to Bhanji Kanji of Kisumu had four sons and three daughters. Sikina Fai, who married Suleman Nurmohamed of Bukoba had four sons and two daughters and Fatma Fai who married Count Jindani of Zanzibar had six daughters, and finally the son, Mohamed.

GROWING UP

THE ROMANCE OF THE REGAL

MY FATHER'S GUN

KENYA AND WORLD WAR II

SHALL WE DANCE?

MY ROLE MODELS

Regal Theatre, also known as
The Regal Cinema

The Regal: I took this picture myself in 1968 from a point diagonally across Salim Road in front of my shop, Badrudin's Sports House.

THE ROMANCE OF THE REGAL

As stated previously, 1931 was an eventful year in the history of the Janmohamed Hasham family, with my birth in Kisumu, on the shores of Lake Victoria, on 6th June, and the death of my grandfather, Janmohamed Hasham, in Mombasa, twelve days later, on 18th June. The other important event of 1931 was the completion of the Regal Cinema building, which was the creation of the two brothers Janmohamed Hasham and Valli Hasham.

The two brothers had been together in business since their early days in Kenya and traded under the name of Valli Hasham & Company. In those days entrepreneurs like Janmohamed and Valli Hasham would usually acquire plots of land and then build houses and shops. To this day I cannot figure out what prompted these two brothers to build a Theatre/Cinema, the very first one in Mombasa, back in 1930/1931. Did they think that Mombasa was ready for a nine hundred seat state of the art theatre? To this day, this has remained an enduring mystery. I will never cease to be astonished at the entrepreneurship and imagination - even the romance - of building a theatre in Mombasa.

We know that the building was designed by a pioneer British architect, William Miller Robertson, who also designed the New Stanley Hotel and the Synagogue in Nairobi. The Regal Theatre building was situated on what was then Salim Road, very near the intersection with Kilindini Road.

The ground floor foot-print of the building consisted of six shops, two with wide frontages onto Salim Road, with a wide foyer entrance with large metal gates which led into the cinema part of the building. The two front shops were tenanted by Husseini Stationery Mart and Edward St. Rose, the chemists. Round the corner from Edward St. Rose, on the

East Street frontage, facing Pandya Building, were the other four shops, two of which were tenanted by Messrs PD Brothers and Messrs DJ Brothers, both of whom were leading makers of bespoke shoes in Mombasa. Another shop was tenanted by Jaffer Pan Walla. On this frontage there were also two wide entrances, one leading to the front stalls seats in the cinema and the other leading up to the Regal Restaurant, which was a spacious restaurant above Husseini Stationery Mart and Edward St. Rose, on the Salim Road frontage.

The cinema hall itself was a very high ceilinged and elegant auditorium, with about five hundred seats on the ground level, and four hundred seats on the upper balcony. The number was reduced later when two separate internal staircases serving the balcony had to be built to comply with new and more stringent fire regulations, following the collapse of the roof of the Naaz Cinema, which was built in 1951, twenty years after the Regal.

Because the Regal was built as a theatre rather than a cinema, it had a stage which was both wide and deep behind the cinema screen, with a large orchestra pit at the front, and a number of dressing rooms for actors and spaces in the wings. The stage was housed in a tall structure to enable scenery and backdrops to be raised and lowered when plays were performed. The stage also had a number of trap doors in the floor, for quick exits and entrances, and in the centre, near the foot-lights was a little cubby-hole, invisible from the audience, from where a "prompt" could help actors who had forgotten their lines!

As a child, my favourite spot in the cinema was easily the projection booth right at the top of the steep balcony, where one could look down at the audience through a number of little square widows which were set at different heights into the wall. We had two enormous 35mm Kelly projectors and a slide projector. The music played before the start of films and during intervals was controlled from there. The records were supplied by Assanand & Sons and Shanker Dass & Sons, who were Mombasa's leading music stores. The arrangement was that they supplied records without charge, and we gave them free publicity and popularised their music by continuous playing in the Theatre. Our three projectionists Tulsi Vithlani, Kurban and Otieno, also controlled the lights, the five minute bell before the film was to start, or to signal the end of the Interval, and of course the opening and closing of the magnificent velvet curtains in front of the movie screen. The projection booth was the nerve centre of the cinema. To me it resembled the bridge of a great ship, with the Captain and his officers controlling what was going to happen next.

One other thing the projectionists were in charge of was the playing of the recorded British National Anthem. Initially the anthem was played at the end of the main feature, when lights would come on, and the audience would stand to attention whilst the anthem was played. The Europeans, mainly British would stand tall and erect. The Indians stood somewhat self-consciously, even sheepishly, because they knew that they were not accepted as real British Subjects, but only, as their Passports stated, as "British Protected Persons" (For the benefit of the uninitiated, persons born in the United Kingdom were "Citizens of United Kingdom" whereas persons born in British Colonies were designated as "British Protected

Persons"Inevitably the divide was racial, because the child of a white Citizen of UK, even though having been born in a colony would still be designated as a Citizen of the UK).

There was also an ambivalence in the indigenous population in those days. There was a large body of opinion which felt that Mombasa and the Coastal strip of Kenya were really part of the domain of the Sultan of Zanzibar, and not part of the British Kenya Colony at all. There were elements in the audiences, particularly in the cheaper front stalls, who would not stand for the anthem but would insultingly walk out, looking with defiance at those who stood to attention. I believe this insulting behaviour was an expression of class envy as much as the then incipient discontent with the colonial masters. This problem was circumvented quite simply by playing the National Anthem before the programme started instead of at the end.

According to Edward Rodwell, "The Regal began receiving a regular supply of excellent shows in 1938 when shows making their way to India would try to meet running expenses at the ports through which they passed. During the second World War, the Regal reached its peak in performances when catering for the many naval and military personnel passing through Mombasa." This also included the provision of an open air cinema for the armed forces. The authorities made available to us a large plot of vacant land exactly behind where the Arch of the Elephant Tusks stands on Kilindini Road today. The Regal used to operate this open air cinema for soldiers and sailors, who, on their way into town from the port, could take in movies if they were so inclined. Any person in uniform could walk in. There were no tickets. All we had to do was to provide the films and the projection facilities.

I especially remember the incredible time in 1955 when La Scala De Milano performed Puccini's *Madame Butterfly* on the Regal stage. The cast of La Scala De Milano were on board the Lloyd Triestino liner MV Europa, en route from Genoa to South Africa. Aficionados like Commander Gibbs, who was the Resident Naval Officer, Ted Stairs who was the Editor of the Mombasa Times, and the Provincial Commissioner, Mr. Desmond O'Hagan, had made overtures to them to give a performance in Mombasa during their four day stopover in Mombasa harbour.

The company's first question was, "Is there a theatre in Mombasa which can handle one of our lavish productions?" The answer was a resounding yes. There was the Regal, which had been built twenty-four years previously by two Indian brothers, Janmohamed and Valli Hasham, which had all the facilities a modern Opera company could desire!

The following write-up in the Daily Nation gives a flavour of the famous occasion.

WHEN AN OPERA TOOK KENYA BY STORM
BY MONTE VIANA

"Cinemas and theatres deal with legends, but sometimes 'show biz' houses become legends in themselves. One such place is Mombasa's Regal Theatre which was the cause one day of the town's major streets being turned into one way lanes and special parking arrangements being made for the night.

East African Airways laid on a special flight to Mombasa and the East African Railways laid on a special train between Nairobi and Mombasa for the occasion.

That was on October 18th 1955. Milan's world famous La Scala Theatre giving a performance of Puccini's Madame Butterfly in Mombasa. Nearly £1,750 was spent on the production and the best seats were sold at £5 and five shillings – the highest ever for a show in Mombasa. Needless to say, it was a red carpet, black-tie affair.

After the opera, the artists agreed that the acoustics of the theatre were 'magnifico'".

As I recall, nearly all the seats were taken by Europeans from all over Kenya. The Regal was the place where all the most important people in the country had to be that evening. One notable non-European at the Regal that evening was the late Mr Habib Keshavjee. Many years later, I asked his son Yusuf to tell me what prompted his father to come to the show. Yusuf Keshavjee's response reads as follows:

"My dear Ameer,

During my childhood in South Africa, our family was always exposed to the opera because of my father's great love for Western classical music. He was exposed to this music from his early days at a Christian school that he attended in Pretoria.

Moreover it was as a result of his viewing some of the movies that he played at his own cinema in Pretoria (Empire) that he was drawn to the opera. His favourites were Verdi's Aida and Puccini's Madame Butterfly.

The music always inspired him and brought up some locked up emotions in his psyche. Perhaps it was also the fact that non-Europeans were denied the right to listen to such wonderful music in live concerts in apartheid South Africa. When we moved to Kenya in 1951 he often talked about the fact that even though Nairobi was not as developed as Johannesburg or Pretoria, our settlement in Kenya would bring us freedoms that were denied to us in South Africa.

You can therefore understand his excitement when in 1955, he heard that there was going to be a live performance of Puccini's Madame Butterfly in Mombasa at a cinema owned by the Janmohamed family!

He made reservations to go by train to Mombasa and bought a ticket at the colossal price of 300/- shillings to attend the gala night. He was probably the only Asian from Nairobi. What a night. When he returned he could not stop talking about the experience. As if this alone justified his move from South Africa to Kenya!!

Yusuf Keshavjee"

The very first show ever at the Regal was a stage production called "King of Jazz" and proved so popular that it was held over for several weeks. In between the regular screening of movies, there were a large number of stage shows which included the D'Oyle Carte Opera Group, *The Nightingale of India Juthika Ray;* and of course *Madame Butterfly;* The Coon Carnival from South Africa; and Wilbur de Paris, an American band leader described as the King of Slip Horn, who fascinated Mombasa audiences with his variety of New Orleans Jazz.

Just a few of the other artists who spring to mind from that time include: a Soiree de Ballet performed by Daphne Dale and Nicole Palajenko, the principal dancers of the International Ballet of the Marquise de Ballet; Trio de Ballet, performed by Ram Gopal of India and two English dancers, Alexis Rassine and Margit Muller; CH Atma; Hemant Kumar; Yusuf Azad; Shakila Banu Bhopali; and Asha Parekh. And then there was Van Shipley, who blew our socks off when we first heard him playing an electric guitar on the Regal stage, using our sound system!

I myself took part in a play on the Regal stage in the early forties. The Aga Khan Schools of Mombasa once staged a variety programme for the public, at the Regal. The programme consisted of several Indian dances, musical items, and an English play, *William Tell*, the immortal tale of the Swiss archer. I was given the role of Walter, his son. The nasty bailiff had commanded my 'father' William Tell (played by Badruddin Hussein Meghji Dossa) to prove his archery skills by shooting an apple placed on my head. My speaking part consisted of keeping my head still and persuading my father not to worry and shoot his arrow to split the apple which was placed on my head. The programme got good reviews in the local press and the next day, the Kenya Daily Mail, saying good things about the evening, singled out my performance for praise. (To this day I am not sure whether the praise was genuine or merely reflected the fact that my family owned the Theatre!)

The Regal auditorium was also used to hold political meetings, most famously when three candidates, A. B. Patel, Dr. Mohamedali Rana, and Kassamali Paroo were contesting the two seats allocated to Coast Asians in Kenya's Legislative Council. Each eligible Asian had two votes to cast. Kassamali Paroo and A. B. Patel were elected on this occasion, the former with a thumping majority. Apparently, most Hindus voted for A. B. Patel and Kassamali Paroo; and most Muslims voted for Dr. M. A. Rana and Kassamali Paroo.

The Regal Theatre Building went up in flames one night in September 1985. The fire started after mid-night, well after the last performance had finished; there was no loss of life or injuries. The very last film which had been shown that evening was an Indian movie called "Chandan ka Palna". The Fire Department were of the opinion that somebody had left a lighted cigarette on an upholstered seat!

Although I lived in London at the time, I learnt about the fire as soon as it took hold. My aunt Sikina Fai (my father's sister) lived on the first floor of City House which was diagonally across from the Regal and had a grandstand view of the conflagration. She phoned me immediately from Mombasa and described to me the destruction of the Regal, even as it was happening. I even heard on the phone, an enormous "whoosh" sound followed by a huge roar. This was the roof of the Regal building coming down, as the flames reached up, deep into the African sky.

It was a gut wrenching moment for her too, for she was witnessing the destruction of an iconic building, a landmark institution which had been built by her father, and my grandfather, Janmohamed Hasham. It must also have been a devastating moment for my father's cousin Ramzan Valli Hasham and my cousin Sultanali Hussein Janmohamed Hasham, who were our two family members who were running the Regal at the time.

But nonetheless, the Regal will live on in the minds of people as a memory, especially in the minds of those who loved it, or had a sense of identification with it. Many others will have fond memories of shows they have seen there.

Picture shows the first African Mayor of Mombasa, Mr. Msanifu Kombo, on the stage of the Regal Theatre, helping me to draw the winning ticket for a Charity raffle during the interval, in a charity film performance at the Regal.

Happily however, and rather improbably, a tangible remembrance of the Regal building exists today, thanks to the sense of historical awareness and initiative of my good friend Sadiq Ghalia. Sadiq is a prominent criminal lawyer in Kenya, a collector of antiques, and is the Hon German Consul in Mombasa. He explained it to me in the following words:

"…One morning I was going to my office, while passing the site of the Regal Cinema I saw it being demolished by a team of African workers. I saw with horror that they were breaking the floor which I knew was covered with beautiful tiles. They were using 'tarimbos'. (Long iron bars with pointed tips at both ends) I stopped my car, walked up to them and requested them to stop the destruction of the tiles and asked them to let me do the job for them. I undertook to remove all the tiles at my cost as soon as possible. Without any resistance, and with incredulous faces they agreed.

So I took my own people there. Carefully removed the tiles. Many were broken in the process. Many were saved. Then began the difficult task of cleaning them. More were broken. After months of hard work under the supervision of Rosemarie what we had were some beautiful antique tiles. These rescued tiles are now affixed in some of the rooms in our home in Nyali where they are admired by all…"

I have been to Sadiq and Rosemarie's home in Nyali. It is a beautiful home on an exceptional site, as it sits atop a cliff facing the Indian Ocean. It also has a surprisingly spacious Gallery/ Museum, rather like an Aladdin's Cave; each hall takes your breathe away, with its collection of rare China, paintings, rugs, Arab doors and various rare artefacts. It is a veritable treasure trove.

And on the floors of some of the rooms, Sadiq and Rosemary have lovingly laid the rescued "Regal" tiles. I have stood on those tiles, and have remembered the three people who must have been the first one to tread upon them, back in 1931. They would have been the brothers Valli Hasham, and Janmohamed Hasham, and William Miller Robertson, the architect, who translated their romantic dream into reality.

My Father's Gun

My father died suddenly and unexpectedly on 9th July 1950 at the age of forty-five of a massive cerebral haemorrhage. I was nineteen then. I had been booked to sail to England at the end of the month, to join the London Polytechnic at the beginning of the new term in September of that year.

A large cabin trunk had been packed in readiness for my impending departure. My proud possession was the Harris Tweed jacket which my father had ordered for me from Ahamed Brothers of Nairobi. I had been briefed on the mysteries of the detachable shirt collar, which enabled students on tight budgets to wear the same shirt for several days, and yet appear with a clean collar under the jacket. And I was given a little pill-box for the studs which went with the detachable collars. One corner of our flat in Mombasa was piled high with tins of biscuits in different shapes and sizes, which friends and relatives had brought as "bhatoo", in the time-honoured Indian custom of bringing a good wishes gifts when somebody was going on a long trip.

All this of course vanished like a puff of smoke when my father first had a stroke and died on the following day. The unthinkable, the unbelievable had happened. The community was in a state of shock. Varasiani Zerabai, first wife of Vazier Fatehali Dhala had also died unexpectedly the day before my father died. Their funerals in fact happened on two succeeding days, and they are buried in adjoining graves in the Ismaili Cemetery in Mombasa.

At the age of nineteen, I had never seen a dead body at close quarters before. This changed when my father died. In those days the ceremonies of "Ghusal" and "Chhanta" were carried out in the homes of the deceased, with male members of the family assisting in the "Ghusal" if a male relative had passed away. And the body was carried in a funeral procession by male members of the community to the cemetery.

(This system changed in Mombasa in 1963 - I was the Kamadia then - when facilities were created in Kuze Jamat Khana for both ceremonies. The practice of funeral processions through the streets of Mombasa was discontinued in 1969 when a hearse was acquired for the transport of the funeral cortege from the Jamat Khana to the cemetery.)

The calamity brought the whole family together and relatives from all over Kenya got together to consider the implications of what had happened. Everybody looked to Manji Motabapa for guidance, as the most senior member of the family. I also remember Badru Mama, my mother's brother, as a pillar of strength at the time.

I do not remember the matter being discussed with me, but it was automatically assumed that my going for further education to England was out of the question. And as Manji Motabapa quite correctly pointed out to me, I not only had to look after the family, I had to get involved in the various business partnerships in which my father had had interests. The thought uppermost in my mind too, was to provide succour and support to my mother and my sisters, and little else mattered. Thus I was totally in agreement that my trip be cancelled.

Just the same, I have often speculated on what would have happened if my father had lived for say another three weeks. I would already have been aboard a ship, bound for a twenty-one day voyage to England. When would I have actually found out about his death? Assuming that I had found out about his death once I reached London, what would have happened next? Would I have been advised to take the next boat back to Mombasa, or would the family have felt that I should continue with my studies since I was already in London? For me this will always remain one, amongst many, of life's "What If?" questions.

My father's funeral took place on what was the 23rd night of Ramadan. With the benefit of hindsight, I came to realise that the numerous religious observances surrounding a death in the family have a cathartic effect on the bereaved family. Some weeks after any bereavement, life slowly has to begin to come back to some semblance of normality as day to day realities impinge on the grief, and demand to be faced. Family members and friends from out of town gradually begin to trickle back to their respective homes, and then finally comes the day when the family finds itself on its own, and that is when the enormity of your loss really hits you. And that is exactly what happened to my mother, Roshan, Sultan and me.

Amongst the hundred and one things we had to deal with, one was to sort out my father's personal effects. Though always immaculate in his cream linen suits, he was not given to extravagance and his wardrobe was quite simple. His only indulgence was the Bridge table. He was a Past President of the Indian Sport Club but he preferred to play Bridge at home. His Bridge foursome consisted of Hussein Jivan Kanji, Hussein Kaloo, Mohamedali Nurmohamed and himself.

I was most fascinated by my father's eclectic collection of books. It consisted of books which he had read whilst he was a student in England in the twenties and thirties. They included "India in Transition" by HH Aga Khan, "Leninism" by Joseph Stalin, "Muhammad – The Prophet" by Mowlana Muhammad Ali, and Hitler's "Mein Kempf". I still have and treasure these books. He also owned the Complete Works of Shakespeare and had a bound set of Classics by Charles Dickens, and some by Sir Walter Scott. His collection was rounded off by books from the time when he was a Law student at Lincoln's Inn, like Salmond on the "Law of Torts, Snell's" "Principles of Equity", and Disney's "Carriage by Railway." But the most astonishing thing I came across as my mother and I went through his personal effects was a gun and a box of cartridges. This was a proper cowboy style revolver with six chambers. I could not, in my wildest flight of fancy, imagine my father having, let alone using, a gun. It was the most unlikely thing to come across in my father's belongings. I remember my father as the most proper and peaceful of men. He could get angry on occasions, but his anger would never lead him to violence. Even the way he used to drive, was non-aggressive and considerate, and many a times as I sat in the back seat of the family Austin Ten, I wished my father would not allow so many people to overtake us.

My mother, however, was able to explain to me the circumstances in which he came to acquire the revolver in the first place. Apparently, in the thirties, during his visits to Kenya, my father was sometimes given the task of going round the Nyanza Province each month by car, collecting cash from various small traders who had bought goods on credit from Valli Hasham & Company, who were major wholesalers and stockists. He was usually accompanied by a guard, but it was considered prudent for him to be armed, for it was generally known that he made this trip each month, and it was obvious that he would have much cash on him towards the end of his trip. There is no record of his ever having had to use his gun!

Once the revolver came into my possession I had an overwhelming desire to fire the gun. I first got Purshotam Bhai of Messrs PD Brothers (our tenants in the Regal Building) to make me a leather holster. One day I took the gun and the box of cartridges and drove to Bamburi, where we had a beach house with several acres of land. I got our caretaker to find an empty Kerosene tin and had it embedded firmly on a sand bank. I put a single bullet in one chamber, took careful aim and fired. There was an almighty bang! I had no idea that a revolver had such a kick, and I have no idea where the bullet went! I realised that no matter how easy it looked in Western movies, this revolver needed to be treated with respect. That was the first and the last time I used the gun.

In the mid nineteen-fifties, during the Mau Mau uprising, the British authorities in Kenya announced that all firearms and ammunition in civilian possession should be handed in immediately to the local police, with severe penalties for non-compliance. This was done to prevent firearms from falling into the hands of the Mau Mau. They said the weapons would be returned to their rightful owners after the Emergency was over.

I was actually quite relieved to hand over the revolver, with the bespoke holster, and the box of cartridges to the Central Police Station in Mombasa. I came home quite shell-shocked after my visit to the Police Station. The police officer who accepted the gun from me inspected it and said it was obvious that it had not been oiled for a very long time, the barrel was rusted inside, and it would probably have blown up the next time it was fired!!!

Kenya And World War II

I was eight when the war broke out and fourteen when it ended. Although World War II started in 1939, the British colony of Kenya only started getting seriously involved when Italy joined up with Hitler in the following year. Italy already had a significant presence in Africa, with colonies in Abyssinia, Eritrea, and more importantly Italian Somaliland, which shared a common, and porous, border with the British Colony of Kenya.

Panic became greater with the fall of France in 1940 which resulted in the former French colony of Madagascar coming under the rule of the Vichy government. Potentially, Kenya was threatened from the North by Italians and from the East by Vichy Madagascar. It was widely believed that it was only a matter of time before Kenya would be attacked; firstly because it was a staging post for British and Commonwealth forces; and secondly, and more importantly, because Mombasa was the finest deep water harbour on the Eastern Seaboard of Africa which provided a base for the Royal Navy, and had dry dock facilities. Whoever controlled Mombasa could effectively command the waters of the western Indian Ocean.

As matter of fact, one of the earliest casualties of the war was the tanker Africa Shell which was sunk in the Mozambique Channel off the coast of East Africa by the German pocket battle-ship Graf Spee right at the beginning of the war.

Once the Japanese bombed the British Naval Base in Trincomalee in Ceylon, the British fleet sailed to Kilindini and Mombasa became the main Naval Base for Allied forces. The British also built a large military depot at Mackinnon Road, forty miles west of Mombasa, on the way to Nairobi. It was then, therefore, that the people of Kenya started preparing for air attacks and even a possible invasion by the Italians and Germans.

We used to live in Nairobi at the outbreak of World War II in 1939. My own earliest memory of the war is the air raid shelter which was dug in the garden of our house on 2nd Parklands Avenue in Nairobi; and for some reason, a big square tin of Huntley & Palmer assorted biscuits. The tin had a light green and orange design on it and it proclaimed that the contents were manufactured in Reading in England. The shelter was built to protect us against air-raids and it was also supposed to accommodate our family of five for many hours, and even days, in case of need, for there was talk of gas attacks. It was equipped with containers of drinking water, candles, blankets, First Aid kits, and non-perishable foodstuffs, along with the tin of biscuits. Roshan, Sultan and I frequently wished for a prolonged air raid warning so that we would all have to stay in the shelter for a while, and perhaps that tin of biscuits would need to be opened. Although there were periodic practices with air raid sirens, Nairobi was never attacked, and I still don't know what finally happened to that tin of biscuits.

The only "hostilities" that I recall in Nairobi were between members of the armed forces passing through Nairobi and the local population. Some of the allied troops, especially the South African soldiers, all white, had disdain for the Asian and African populations of Nairobi, and appeared to think that all dusky women were fair game. The Military Police tried to maintain some semblance of control, but soldiers seemed to have unbridled licence to behave pretty much as they wanted to. After patriotically putting up with abuse for some time, and after seeing their numerous representations to the civil authorities being ignored, the Asian community of River Road in Nairobi (many of whom lived above or near their shops) decided to take matters in their own hands and formed vigilante patrols to protect their women and children from the soldiers. If memory serves, an important member of the organisation was a Mr. Thuman Singh, a sweetmeat (mithai) seller, who was also a champion professional wrestler.

Over a period of time, clashes took place regularly when soldiers ventured into River Road, and the locals armed with hockey sticks usually came out on top. Several marauding and usually inebriated soldiers were beaten up on River Road. Eventually the authorities thought it prudent to accede to the request of the Asian shopkeepers. River Road was declared out of bounds to all WD personnel. There was little point in soldiers acquiring broken bones without having yet encountered a single German, Italian or Japanese.

I cannot understand what attracted the soldiers to River Road in the first place. There were no bright lights; there were no bars, and there were no brothels. That is not to say that there was no prostitution in the Asian community at the time. But in keeping with Indian cultural constraints, this was conducted with discretion and a certain amount of finesse. You would not find Indian girls standing on street corners, flaunting their wares. Ladies of easy virtue would be known to certain "carers" who would in turn arrange assignations, and the cognoscente would know how to contact the "carers", who were at times elderly women.

Welfare of the troops is of course a major consideration in times of war. It was recognised that sailors who had been to sea for long stints and soldiers from distant lands who had been away from their homes for long periods - and who were prepared to lay down their lives for their country - had to be provided with diversions, which included female companionship.

Mombasa in particular became a magnet for unattached indigenous ladies, especially when the fleet was in. Bus loads of girls from upcountry descended on Mombasa. Given the secrecy which surrounded troop movements, I still haven't worked out how girls from up-country knew when allied warships were going to be in port at any given time. I suspect that the Navy quietly had the services of "liaison officers" who arranged for bus loads of girls to be in Mombasa at the same time as the ships of the Royal Navy.

Mombasa's Medical Officer of Health and the Port Health Authority operated a screening service for all "girls" who were required to undergo periodic physical check-ups to ensure that they were not carrying any diseases. Those who had a clean bill of health carried a little "pass" which enabled them to frequent bars and other places popular with soldiers and sailors. Names like the Star Bar, and the Bristol, and the Britannia spring to mind. Checks were randomly carried out by the Military Police and the Shore Patrol. Any "girl" without a valid "pass" would be shoo'd away.

On one occasion, during a check-up one of the regular "girls" was found to have picked up some form of venereal disease. (AIDS was unknown then.) She appeared to have picked it up from a sailor from one of the ships. When questioned she could not describe him. She only remembered him as "Johnny". The Port Authority worked out the names of the several ships which were in port around that time the "girl" had had the encounter with "Johnny". A signal was sent to the suspect ships. The offending sailor was actually located on one of the ships. He was isolated in the sick bay and denied shore leave until he underwent treatment for his problem. The "girl" was meanwhile treated in Mombasa, and had her "pass" taken away.

My other memory of the war years is the blackout. I remember my father taking turns to patrol Parklands Avenue in Nairobi some evenings each week to ensure that black-out was properly observed. He was a member of the ARP. All glass windows were criss-crossed with sticky tape to prevent them from shattering.

And there was petrol rationing, and petrol coupons. My father had a green Austin Ten. He used the Austin for nearly seven years because no cars were imported for civilian use during the war years. Limited importation of cars for civilian use only began in 1946/7, but then cars were only allocated to people who had some sort of priority. My father qualified for a new Ford Prefect since he was a Municipal Councillor and a member of the Rent Control Board in Mombasa.

The three brothers, Manji, Hussein and my father Kassam Janmohamed separated in business towards the end of 1940. Manji Motabapa kept the Nairobi business and properties. Hussein Motabapa and my father kept the Mombasa assets which included the Regal Theatre, City House and some other properties. We thus moved to Mombasa during the early stages of war (1941/1942) and rented an apartment in a building between the Goan Institute and the Masonic Lodge on Mbaraki Road, leading towards the Likoni ferry. It had four flats and was referred to as "Nehra Building", named after the owner. We stayed there for nearly ten years, during which time we had a number of nice neighbours in the other three apartments. These included the families of David Owen-Thomas, Purshotambhai of PD Bros, Chhotubhai–Ismail Mohamed Jaffer, who had recently arrived from India, Mrs. Malekbai Janu Hussein Suleman Verjee, Shaban Gulamali, Abdul Tharani, and Hussein Valli Essa, among others.

Preparations for war were much more evident in Mombasa than in Nairobi. But then, Mombasa as the Naval Base, was under much greater threat than Nairobi, which is three hundred miles inland. The reason, of course, was the presence of thousands of sailors, from Destroyers, Cruisers, Troop Transports, Air-craft Carriers, Submarines and Mine-Sweepers. This was in addition to the British and other soldiers from Australia, New Zealand, India, South Africa, America and of course, the KAR, King's African Rifles, which was a British colonial regiment raised from various British possessions in Eastern Africa.

During the war the KAR rank and file soldiers were always Africans, whilst officers were Europeans, seconded from British army regiments. They looked rather splendid, in their khaki uniforms and Fez caps, and a red cummerbund on ceremonial occasions; and they marched well and had their own band which played stirring martial music. They had a rousing marching song which went something like this:

Twende, Twende,
Safari Ya Ulaya,
Shawri ya Bwana, ho ho,
Shawri ya Bwana.

Loosely translated it means:

Let us go, let us go, (or come on, come on),
On a trip to Europe,
(for the) Purpose (or cause) of the bwana, ho ho,
Purpose of the bwana.
(Bwana could mean Boss, Master, Employer or Mister)

Soldiers of the Kings African Rifles saw action in Abyssinia, against the Italians, and the Vichy French in Madagascar, and the Japanese in the jungles of Burma.

They would have seen a number of things during these forays. They would have seen why the "Bwanas" ruled their country; they would have seen that the Bwanas were better trained, better equipped, and were disciplined. They would have seen white people killing each other on the front lines. And they would have noticed that, whether wounded by bullets, bayonets or shrapnel, all soldiers bled red.

The island of Mombasa was festooned with anti-aircraft batteries, surrounded by sand-bags; and there were search-light emplacements, with fingers of light probing the starlit African nights, making eerie patterns in the skies when there were clouds about. And there were gun emplacements on the Light-house and Likoni sea-fronts, camouflaged to look like Baobab tree-trunks. Some of the brick-work still exists.

Even though I was only just approaching my teens, I could not help noticing the presence of a large number of what I thought were amazingly pretty young women, in smart white or khaki uniforms with pert little caps on their heads. These were the members of the WRENS, and the WRACS, and the FANNIES, which were the women's auxiliary services, who had come out from England to provide support services for the troops. They served as nurses, drove ambulances and limousines, did secretarial duties and generally looked after the welfare of the troops. And I also remember the despatch riders, going about importantly on their Ariel and Match-less motor-bikes. That was the first time I saw motor-cyclists wearing crash helmets and goggles. They carried khaki canvas bags in which they kept their gas masks and their despatches. There was also a spate of large American cars which suddenly appeared on the streets of Mombasa, for use by high ranking officers, and always driven by attractive female drivers, who jumped out of the driver's seat to open the doors for their officer passengers, and saluted them smartly. The cars were mostly Dodges, Plymouths, Chryslers and Chevrolets. Despite the fact that they were all painted khaki, they made quite a change from the more sedate and smaller English cars which we were used to seeing on the roads of Kenya. The top of the range English cars on our roads until then were Humbers, especially the Super Snipe model, much favoured by the Government House and the Resident Naval Officer, and other VIPs. On a lower scale there were the Humber Hawks, Hillmans, Fords, Austins, Vauxhalls, Morris and so on.

There was good reason for English cars to be so popular. In those days, any manufactured item which had the "Made in England" label was highly regarded. Apart from the fact that Kenya, as a British Colony, had greater exposure to British imports, British manufactured goods had proved themselves to be of first rate quality. My father used his Austin Ten for nearly ten years, and I don't remember too many times when the car went into a garage. Although it must be said, the way my father drove and looked after his car, it would probably have lasted him twenty years.

Those were fascinating days for me. My mind had been conditioned by war and adventure films, and the Gaumont British News and Movietone Newsreels I used to see frequently in our own cinema, the Regal. And I subscribed to the Boys Own magazine and other adventure publications. I had a romanticised picture of war, deeds of heroism, people laying down their lives for their country, and so on. And I had this fascination with the tools of war, like ships, planes, various forms of military transport, guns, and so on.

As if my prayers had been answered, the large open field directly in front of our flat in Nehra building was commandeered by the authorities, where a huge amount of construction took place. Firstly, they built a NAAFI canteen; then they built a large hall, called the Garrison Theatre; and to protect all this, they installed gun emplacements and search-light units.

Inevitably, this resulted in increased comings and goings of uniformed soldiers, sailors, despatch riders, with their goggles and crash helmets, and officers in their American cars with their pretty drivers, and others. I used to spend a lot of stolen hours on the terrace in front of our house, watching with fascination all this activity, identifying various makes of cars and motor-bikes which came and went. And there was continuous playing of music in the NAAFI canteen. This would start at noon and go on until late at night. I became familiar with all the current hits. The one that seemed to be most popular went something like this:

> *You are my sunshine, my only sunshine;*
> *You make me happy, when skies are grey.*
> *You never notice how much I love you,*
> *Please don't take my sunshine away.*

Then came the bad news one day. The Allies were losing the war in North Africa. Rommel and his troops were heading towards Egypt. It was decided that the island of Mombasa would have to be evacuated of all non-essential civilian residents. Aerial attacks were imminent.

A family friend, and distant relative of ours, Mr. Shivji Nurmohamed used to own a house in Likoni. (His wife Kamar was the daughter of Jiwa Hasham Verjee.) It was about two or three miles past the Likoni ferry, on mainland south. Our whole family, including my grandmother Mrs. Panbai Janmohamed, and the entire Hussein Janmohamed family moved into this house for the duration.

Oh, what excitement! My father and one of my cousins Shamsuddin Hussein Janmohamed used to go into Mombasa each day. They had the family businesses, including the Regal, to tend. There was much relief when they came back each evening, because frequent gun-fire and explosions could be heard during the daytime, even three miles inland in Likoni, and we could not tell whether this was practice firing or whether Mombasa was under the long expected aerial bombardment by the Italian air force.

Amongst other memories, my abiding memory of this stay in Likoni was a ritual which I was privileged to perform each evening, when the sun went down and kerosene lamps were lit, with the hiss of the occasional Petromax lamp which became the brightest spot around.

On the Equator of course there is not much of a dawn or dusk. One minute it is dark and suddenly it is day as the sun quite quickly emerges from beyond the horizon. Night comes equally dramatically. All my young life, I was the favourite of my uncle Hussein Janmohamed. He used to enjoy his Dimple Scotch (in the triangular bottle) with soda each evening. He had his table and chairs outside, under a mango tree. He himself lounged on a deck-chair. His favourite attire was a Kikoi and a vest. And he liked to listen to Indian records whilst he savoured his drinks. The 78 rpm records were played on a gramophone ("His Master's Voice" as I remember). As his favourite nephew, it was my privilege to wind the gramophone before each record could be played. Each record played for about three minutes and the gramophone had to be wound before each record. His favourite record was "Piya Milan Ko Jana" ("Going to Meet Your Beloved") which he wanted to hear over and over again every evening, and as I recall, I had a lot of exercise turning the handle of the gramophone each evening. It was a privilege for me to be asked to do that, and I recall envy and jealousy from my cousins and sisters.

I had a special place for Hussein Motabapa in my heart. He had been my surrogate father when my own father was still studying in England. I can vividly remember the look of contentment on his face when he had his first drink of the evening and the record was playing Pankaj Malik, singing his favourite song. He would occasionally rub his palms together in satisfaction. I think of him sometimes when I sit down myself, on an evening in front of my own TV, with a glass of Famous Grouse in my hands. Like him, I too like my Scotch with soda. Now I know how he felt. He passed away in 1947.

After a few months in Likoni, our family had to move once again. This time we were sent to Kisumu, five hundred miles inland. It entailed an overnight train journey to Nairobi, and then a further two hundred mile train journey to Kisumu. For some reason I don't have many memories of our short stay in Kisumu, except that we stayed at the house of our Bhani Fai, my father's sister. She was a formidable lady who ran a family business called Janmohamed Silk Store in Kisumu. The family lived in spacious accommodation behind the shop.

There was no electricity in Kisumu during those days, so lanterns were the order of the day. We slept on mattresses on the floors, under room-sized, tent-like mosquito nets suspended from ceilings. Each evening, after the rooms had been sprayed with Fly Tox pumps the netting would be unfurled to protect us from the virulent Lake Victoria mosquitoes.

I remember that I had been enrolled at the local Government Indian School. The only thing I remember about that school has nothing to do with education. During recess and at the end of school, a lady used to sit outside the school gates selling Vadas. She was affectionately known as Mama Khalele. And to this day, I swear that I have never tasted better Vadas and chatni in my life. I know that many have tried but nobody has ever successfully replicated Mama Khalele's Vadas. She took her secret to the grave - may her soul rest in peace.

We were in Kisumu for some months only before it was considered safe for us to return to Mombasa, for the tide of war seemed to be turning. Rommel's forces had been defeated and the Germans were in retreat. Monty had turned the tide.

One of the mysteries of the Second World War is that the only place in East Africa where bombs were apparently dropped was Malindi, seventy miles north of Mombasa. Apparently, Italian air force planes dropped three bombs on Malindi one fine day, met with no ground fire or any resistance, did little or no damage, and returned north from whence they came. The story is that they either mistook Malindi for Mombasa, or perhaps, more plausibly, had been on an Indian Ocean patrol, were running out of fuel, and decided to dump their bombs on any sign of civilisation they could find, before returning to their base. In any case, they never returned.

One day the war in Europe was over, followed by the capitulation of Japan. The war had left no physical scars on Kenya. In fact there was a lot of development. Certainly there had begun a gentle breeze which eventually turned into what Harold McMillan would one day describe as the "winds of change".

A legacy of the war years was a number of first class tarmac roads which were built. Firstly there was a ten mile stretch, near the army base in Mackinnon Road. This was forty miles west of Mombasa, on the road to Nairobi. Then there was the fifty mile stretch between Moshi and Arusha in Tanganyika. This was built by Polish refugees who had been housed in a refugee camp near Lake Duluti. They were among the very large number of Poles who managed to escape with their families from Poland when the Germans invaded their country. Another amazing Polish feat of engineering was the construction of the tarmac road on the Escarpment, between Nairobi and Naivasha. It is one of the most picturesque routes imaginable, as the road zigzags down the Escarpment into the Rift Valley.

SHALL WE DANCE?

Sometime in 1951 a young man called Amir Gangji, disembarked from a British India Steam Navigation Company ship which docked in Kilindini harbour, having arrived from Zanzibar. He was the son of Count Abdulla Hasham Gangji, a prominent Ismaili leader, based in Zanzibar. He had been sent to gain greater experience in business and was apprenticed to the African Ivory Company, which used to operate from the Old Town in Mombasa.

The gifted Amir brought with him many attributes and qualities. The foremost being his sociable and gregarious nature. As Count Gangji's son he was known to all the foremost families in Mombasa. There would hardly be a party in Mombasa where Amir would not be invited. He had an uncanny resemblance to Omar Shariff. He was also recognised as a very eligible bachelor. Amir also happened to be an excellent ball-room dancer. He had learnt to dance in Zanzibar and had a tremendous sense of rhythm. His Tango was a pleasure to behold. His one regret was that there was nowhere for him to dance in Mombasa. No Ismailis, or many Indians for that matter, knew how to dance in Mombasa at the time. The only Asian community which danced were the Goan community. It has often been said – with some envy - that if you settle a community of Goans anywhere in the world, they will create a Church, a school, and a Goan Institute – for their social and sporting needs. True to form, Mombasa had all three.

I used to play in the Aga Khan Club badminton team and we frequently exchanged visits with the Goan Institute. These matches were normally arranged for Sunday mornings, with play commencing at seven in the morning. The matches would last some hours, and this was followed by the host Club providing refreshments. The Aga Khan Club refreshments usually consisted of jalebi ganthia tea and soft drinks, served in the Diamond Jubilee Hall. The GI did things somewhat differently. After play, we would all repair to the hall which occupied the first floor, and refreshments would consist of sandwiches, samosas, tea, coffee, soft drinks and beers. There was always music, sometimes recorded, often live because the Goans were a musically gifted people and many of them could pick up an instrument and make music.

I mention all this because it was at one such occasion that I danced for the first time in my life. I was 20. The matches were over and we were at the upstairs hall in the GI. Somebody struck up dance music and all our Goan friends were on the floor. None of the Ismailis joined in.

I am trying to remember the names of the girls who played on our team. There were the two Khatoons, Khatoon Paroo and Khatoon Javer. (Khatoon Javer and I were the winners of the Najma Cup for Mixed Doubles in 1949). There were the two sisters, Rozina and Roshan Karim Esmail. Then there was Guli PD, Shahsultan Haji Mitha, Roshan Bhimji, and of course our two player/chaperones Malek Chachi and Zeinub Rashid. None of them danced. The leading light of the GI team was Cissy Pereira. She was an excellent badminton player, an all-round athlete, and the life and soul at parties. Seeing that none of the Aga Khan Club players were on the floor, she came up to me (I used to speak on behalf of our team) and absolutely insisted that I dance with her. She brushed aside my protestations that I did not even know how to. She said she had never felt so insulted - and finally persuaded me to go on the floor with her by accusing me of ungentlemanly behaviour.

Dear Cissy! Wherever you are now, I shall never forget that first dance of my life. I was in white shorts and a Fred Perry shirt, you wore a white shirt and short pleated skirt. We were both sweaty after the match, with sticky palms, and you asked the musicians to play an easy Samba for my benefit as you led me through my first ever steps to music. You had taken off your tennis shoes because they don't slide easily on a wooden floor. I refused to do the same because I was not sure if my socks were free of holes.

There was already an Ismaili dance club in Nairobi. It was called the Pomegranate Club, and it had been started by the irrepressible Badru Eboo. I have been given to understand that Daressalaam also had an Ismaili dance club called the "21 Club".

That was the situation when Amir Gangji appeared on the scene. He would frequently question why the otherwise quite progressive Ismaili youngsters in Mombasa did not dance. He brought the idea of forming a club to me. Instigated by Amir Gangji, six of us, namely Amir Gangji, the two sisters Nurjehan and Gulshan Verjee (both of whom could dance), Amir Premji Dhanji, Abdul Valli and myself became what may be described as the Founder Members of the Club. In 1952 we decided to take the plunge and formed our first Managing Committee. I was chosen as the President, Amir Gangji took over as the Hon. Secretary and Taj Dhala became the Hon. Treasurer. We had Guli Fatehali Dhala, Gulshan

The Founder Members of the Lido Club, 1952. Left to right Amir P. Dhanji, Gulshan Verjee, Amir Gangji, Ameer Janmohamed, Nurjehan Verjee and Abdul Valli.

Picture shows first managing committee consisting of Abdul Valli, Guli Fatehali, myself as the President, Taj Dhala as the Hon. Tresasurer, Gulshan Verjee and Amir Gangji as Hon. Sec.

Verjee and Abdul Valli as committee members.

My first wife Munira and I had recently returned from a European holiday and had come back with fond memories of the Lido in Paris. I suggested we call our club the Lido Club. This was accepted. We found ourselves a suitable venue, which was in the Little Theatre Club premises on Ganjoni Road. And we decided to have a dance every month.

So, we had a club, we had a name, and we had a venue. The problem was that only one or two of us could dance. We were introduced to an English couple, Mr. and Mrs. James, who agreed to give us dancing lessons. They used to charge us by the hour, and we danced to scratchy 78 rpm (revolution per minute) gramophone records where each piece of music lasted for two and a half minutes. We also had an extremely amiable Goan band leader called Abel Correa who would provide us with "sympathetic" music, suitable for a bunch of raw learners, with stiff movements and little sense of rhythm.

There was strong opposition within the community. There was at least one Missionary who spoke up at Jamati gatherings and he condemned the club as an "evil" which had been introduced into the community. He asked how respectable men could allow their wives and daughters and sisters to dance in the arms of other men. He conjured up pictures of debauchery and shamelessness. Fortunately for us, we had the support of some senior

Mr. Ramzan Jamal addressing Anniversary Dinner at the Diamond Juibilee Hall. Committee Members Shamsu Suleman Damji, Mithoo Premji Dhanji and Sultan Cassam in the background on the Committee Table.

members of the Community. I think it was because of Amir Gangji that Count Fatehali Dhala not only allowed Guli and Amin to take a leading part in the club, he also became a member. His joining the club was a signal for other not so young Ismaili couples to join the club. They were Dr. & Mrs. Lalani, Mr. & Mrs. Badrudin Alibhai Kanji, Mr. & Mrs. Jafferali KS Meghji, Mr. & Mrs. Mohamedali Rashid, Mr. & Mrs. Tadin Jessani, Mr. & Mrs. Ramzan Hussein Meghji Dossa, and Mr. & Mrs. Kassamali K Premji. Count Fatehali did not come on the floor, but all the others did, and it is to their credit that many of them even took dancing lessons.

Once people started to learn ballroom dancing, they wanted to practice more and more. The Lido Club only had one function each month. There were not too many places in Mombasa where Indians could go to dance. Some of us resorted to going on board passenger ships which were docked in Kilindini Harbour. They often had orchestras playing in the evenings, and we could dance without being too self-conscious. We also had parties at home and would dance to gramophone records.

So, Amir Gangji and I may take credit - and blame if any - for the formation of the Lido Club in Mombasa, but one thing is pretty certain. It would not have survived had it not been for the support of Count Fatehali and his friends who gave the Lido Club the respectability it needed.

My committee and I finished our term of office with the Club in good health, and it is a measure of our success that no less a person than Mr. Ramzan Hasham Jamal took over the Presidency of the Lido Club from me.

My Role Models

As a young man in Kenya, there were three persons especially whom I admired most, and I felt it would be good if I could be like them as I grew up. All three of them were doing different things in life, but each had qualities which I deeply admired and wished to emulate.

These three role models were: Count Kassamali Paroo, Anant Pandya and Hassan Rattansi. All three were scions of reputable families.

COUNT KASSAMALI PAROO

The first time I really noticed Kassamali Paroo was when he was contesting a seat in Kenya's Legislative Council. Two Asian seats had been specifically allocated to the Coast Province. Three candidates, Ambalal Patel, Dr. Mohamedali Rana and Kassamali Paroo were contesting the two seats. Voters had to elect two members to represent them in Kenya's new Legislature.

I especially remember the way Kassamali Paroo could address crowds of people, in English and in Gujarati, with equal facility, his manner of speech, his personality, his general deportment, and gravitas – all made a lasting impression on me. Though short in stature, he walked with long strides.

After all the speech making was over, the final casting of votes and the counting happened in the Kaderbhoy Hall in Makadara. Paroo was elected with a thumping majority. The arithmetic was simple. Most Hindus gave their first vote to A.B.Patel and their second vote to Paroo. Likewise, most Muslims gave their first vote to Dr. Rana and their second to Paroo.

I also observed him as the President of the Ismaili Provincial Council in Mombasa. Also as the Managing Director of the Jubilee Insurance Company and the Diamond Jubilee Investment Trust. He frequently addressed the Jamat on various matters - he was also an honorary waezeen and every time I thought he talked convincingly, without hyperbole or histrionics, and conducted himself extremely well.

Kassamali Paroo was a keen Bridge player and a regular at the Indian Sports Club. I used to see him most days on the front veranda of the Club, holding court, so to speak, with other regulars like Dr. Hassan, Hassanali Datoo, Mohamed Hussein Nasser (Congo), Badru Mussa Jetha, Abdul Malik Alibhai Kanji, and others. He seldom ventured into 'my' areas of the club, which were the Billiards room and the Rummy sections of the club. I had begun to learn Bridge but could not even contemplate making up a fourth on a table with Count Paroo.

However, I got to know him a lot better when I became a Rotarian. Despite the disparity in our ages, I believe we even developed a special rapport. He would frequently talk to me about olden days whenever I visited Mombasa from London. He sometimes spoke to me about the time when my father and he were students in Gondal in India around 1918. We used to sit on a bench in the front courtyard of Kuze Jamat Khana since both of us always used to be early arrivals. He took delight in introducing me to new Ismailis who had settled in Mombasa after I left for the UK. He would tell the new arrivals to read the names of the past Mukhis and Kamadias in the Jamat Khana entrance hall.

His first wife was Mani, an elegant and attractive lady of the frock and pachhedi generation. Yes, he was a fine man. The passage of time has not dimmed my admiration for him, and I still acknowledge him as one of my Role Models.

ANANT PANDYA

I used to think that Anant had everything a man could desire in life. He was born into a distinguished Brahmin family. His family was well known in India and in East Africa. They were big time hardware importers and also published a bi-lingual newspaper called the Kenya Daily Mail, which had a wide circulation, especially amongst those who could not read English. The Pandya Memorial Clinic in Mombasa was one of their numerous charities.

Anant himself was a tall, good looking fellow with a natural swagger, which sat well with him. He was educated at the Alidina High School in Mombasa, and then did a degree in Economics and Political Science at the London School of Economics, followed by Bar-at-Law at Lincoln's Inn. His wife was called Hansa. Hansa Bahen was one of the most beautiful Indian women I can think of. Although she was a university graduate, and spoke excellent English, there was an uncompromising Indian-ness about her. I have never seen her in western dress; she always wore saris. She wore chappals on her feet and always had a prominent red tilak on her forehead.

Anant's personality, his ability to speak in public, combined with his family background and financial independence more or less made it inevitable that he would go into public life. The number of bodies he served on would fill pages. It would be fair to say that there was hardly a worthwhile public body on which he had not served, including the Kenya Legislature.

Although I had belonged with him on the Asian Sports Board and the United Kenya Club, I really got to know him better when I became a Rotarian in 1956. He was already a highly respected Rotarian when I joined. He had his sights set on becoming the Governor of our Rotary District. No non-European had ever held the office. He got elected to the post in

1965 - Anant and Hansa Pandya, and Zeenat and myself, receive the Attorney General of Kenya, Hon. Charles Njonjo, at Port Reitz Airport. He was the Principal Guest and Keynote Speaker at Anant Pandya's District Conference in Mombasa.

1965 and he holds the distinction of being the first non-European Rotary District Governor in sub-Saharan Africa. (I was the second one to do so in 1969). The two of us worked quite closely during his term as DG, for I was the President of the Mombasa Rotary Club which hosted his District Conference in Mombasa.

I have spoken to Rotary Clubs in many parts of the world, but more often than not, somebody would come up to me and ask me if I "knew a chap called Anant Pandya who came from the same part of the world as you"!

HASSAN RATTANSI

Last, but by no means least, is dear Hassan Rattansi because he was gifted with the best attributes of both Kassamali Paroo and Anant Pandya. I got to know Hassan rather well because his first wife Gulzar and my first wife Munira were sisters. We were both in the sports goods business, he in Nairobi and I in Mombasa. He also had additional qualities which were unique to him. For one thing, he was an excellent sportsman, played Cricket and Tennis for Kenya, and officiated as Team Manager when Kenyan Teams went abroad to take part in international events. He was also Chairman of the Asian Sports Association of Kenya, Kenya Lawn Tennis, Kenya National Sports Council etc.

A man with rugged good looks, his physique reflected the fitness and weight training which he used to do. The thing which really impressed me about him however was his sense of humour. He was not a public orator in the Paroo or Pandya mould. However, he could hold groups of people spellbound with his conversational skills, his use of words, both in English and Gujarati. He particularly excelled as an after-dinner speaker, and his brand of humour is legendary. I remember him as one of the most popular and universally liked individuals I have been privileged to know.

I used to meet people of all races and political persuasions at his house in Nairobi. Amongst so many other interesting people, I was privileged to make the acquaintance of Tom Mboya and Charles Njonjo, who was their family friend. Our son Quassim often used to spend his half-terms at the Njonjo farm when he was at the Prince of Wales (now Nairobi) school in Nairobi.

Charles Njonjo (former Attorney General of Kenya) had the following to say about Hassan in a tribute printed in the Awaaz magazine in 2004, "*Hassan is an extraordinary man. I don't think in my life I have met a man who you meet for the first time and you feel an affinity towards him. In 1962 I returned from England as a young lawyer and was employed by the Kenya government. I had a job but nowhere to stay. The residential areas were strictly segregated with Europeans in Karen and Westland suburbs, the Asians in Parklands and the Africans in the slum areas. Hassan heard about my predicament and without a second thought, invited me into his home. I stayed with him for two months before I moved to spend another two months with Sir*

*Hassan Rattansi with
my first wife Munira,
and his first wife Gulzar,
in London in summer of
1954. Munira and Gulzar
were sisters.*

*Hassan and
myself in
Southend-on-Sea,
in England, 1954.*

Ernest Vasey before I was finally given a government house just opposite the State House.

Hassan was a remarkably open and cosmopolitan thinker. He, together with Ibrahim Nathoo, John Mutura, Derrek Erskine, myself and others formed the United Kenya Club."

Hassan also had a passion for sporting cars. He was amongst the first ones to acquire the new Saab Coupe when it came to Kenya, also the first Audi Coupe.

Education and Innovation

THE IMPORTANCE OF EDUCATION

Looking back at the history of our wider family, going back five generations, to great great great grandfather Verjee (or Virjee as his name would have been pronounced in Gujarati then), one of the astonishing decisions taken by four of his grandsons, namely, Hussein Suleman Verjee, Madatali Suleman Verjee, Kassam Suleman Verjee and my grandfather Janmohamed Hasham Verjee, was to send their sons, first to India, and then to England for further education, back in 1918.

Since migrating to Africa from India in the late 19th century, both Suleman Verjee and the Hasham Verjee families had done well for themselves in trade and commerce. The Suleman Verjee boys especially, made a name for themselves in public life and politics in colonial Kenya. Many public buildings and institutions in pre-independence Kenya used to bear their names in testimony of their involvement and generosity.

According to Hassanali Kaka's diary, the Verjee family received a back-handed compliment from the Danish writer Karen Blixen, in her book "Out of Africa". She writes, "The Indians of Nairobi dominated the big Native business quarter of the Bazaar and the great Indian merchants had their little villas just outside the town; Jivanjee, Suleman Verjee, Allidina Visram…they gave tea parties in their gardens with Indian pastries…they were clever, travelled and highly polite people. But the Indians in Africa are such grasping tradesmen that with them you would never know if you were face to face with a human individual or with the head of a firm…"

One can only conjecture about how the decision to send the boys away from home for further education was arrived at. There would have been logistical problems too, since as their horizons expanded, the family had started to diversify and do things independently, quite often in competition with each other. How did the idea originate?

Several possibilities spring to mind. It is conceivable that during one of his visits to Africa, Mowlana Sultan Mohamed Shah would have granted an audience to members of the family, and might have planted the idea of educating the boys abroad. At the same time, Madatali Suleman Verjee was, in 1918, the Chairman of what must have been one of the earliest, if not the very first, Aga Khan Education Boards in Kenya. This is significant because the formation of that Education Board in 1918 was the beginning of the creation of the Aga Khan Schools network in Kenya. Education was beginning to gain in importance in the minds of the now successful Indian merchants, traders and property owners. But at this time, Asian children had little choice but to attend Mission Society Schools. It is not at all surprising, therefore, that the brothers Kassam, Madatali and Hussein Suleman Verjee were minded to do better - to procure the best education for their sons. It is tempting too, to speculate that Madatali Suleman Verjee was the one who played an important role in the plans to send these Verjee boys away to achieve that aim.

More detailed information about the story of the Aga Khan Schools follows in "Aga Khan High".

AT SCHOOL IN INDIA

We know that my father was first sent to India. Very little information is available on this particular aspect of his education, except for the fact that in one legal document, my grandfather, Janmohamed Hasham describes himself as, "I, Janmohamed Hasham, of Junagadh State..." Junagadh is not too many miles from Gondal, and although our family had moved to Kenya from 1895 onwards, my grandfather would have known about the reputation of the schools in Gondal.

As it happened, (Count) Kassamali Paroo, of Mombasa, was also a student in the same school in India at the same time, and later he went on to recount his experiences meticulously in an interesting journal, and I quote:

"..... the (1914/1918) war was still on and I was only eleven years old, in spite of which my father took me with him to Gondal, in India, to Garassia College. Thus we travelled

Kassam Janmohamed: In school uniform in Gondal, India in 1918.

59

to India in February 1917 and stayed in Bombay for a few days and we then proceeded to Gujarat. Here, at Garassia College I was left to study. Although Garassia was called a college, the level of education was only up to Matriculation.

..... in Kathiawar, Rajkot, there was also a college called Raj Kumar. This was considered the best college in India. Second to this was Garassia. Students here were mostly sons of Rajas. Here there were Hindu scholars and some Muslim students too. When I was enrolled at Garassia College, there were other Ismaili students, who were:

> *Badruddin Kara Teja*
> *Kassam Janmohamed*
> *Two sons of Ismail Simbha*

They were in the second and third years. Then came some other boys and Janubhai, my brother-in-law ... After one term, they all left. This was because they could not stand the food that was served. Each term was four and a half months, and vacation lasted one and a half month. No meat or fish was served during term time as the College was strictly vegetarian. Students were not allowed to eat non-vegetarian food even outside school.

..... up to the third class I was in Gondal. I was not always first in class, but definitely stood second. A Mombasa resident, called Kassam Janmohamed was in my class. Looking back at life, Kassam Janmohamed was a director with me in Jubilee Insurance. He was also a member of the Ismaili Provincial Council. He was always very astute in his studies ...

And Count Paroo went on to write;

... in June/July 1920 Abdulhusssein (Abdulrasul Alidina Visram) and I boarded the boat (from Mombasa) "Loyalty Sindhiani" and we set off for England. As luck would have it, on this boat there were also five Suleman Verjee's boys, also on their way to England:

> *Nazarali Madatally Suleman Verjee*
> *Rajabali Kassam Suleman Verjee*
> *Hassanalli Hussein Suleman Verjee*
> *Gulamali Madatally Suleman Verjee*
> *Rahemtulla Kassam Suleman Verjee*

Kassamali Paroo and the Verjee cousins parted company once they arrived in England, for I understand that Count Paroo went to the Torfield School in Eastbourne 1920/1922 and then Saint Paul School 1922-1924.

VERJEE BOYS AT BRYNMELYN

The Verjee cousins went to Brynmelyn School in Weston-Super-Mare. I understand that it was an inexpensive school even by the standards of the day. Boarders paid between 24 and 28 guineas per term. And, every boarder was expected to have at least three pence a week pocket money.

According to Hassanali Hussein Suleman Verjee in his journal "Pioneers in East Africa – The Verjee Family", Brynmelyn School, Weston-Super-Mare, had been recommended by a Mr.Soper who used to act as an agent for Suleman Verjee & Sons in London. He goes on to write:

> *"I found life in England difficult at first. The cold weather came as a shock, and I spoke very little English. I had to adapt to a completely different life-style, even different eating habits. As in all English Public Schools, new boys were forced to undergo a brutal 'initiation' ritual. At Brynmelyn, the preferred rite was humiliating as well as painful – getting one's bare bottom scorched in front of a fire."*

We next read about the Verjee cousins in the book, "Landon of Brynmelyn" by Olive Hallam. This is both a history of Brynmelyn School, in Weston-Super-Mare, in England, and of one Henry Ernest Landon, (Olive Hallam's father) who was the Headmaster of the School. He was keen on Association Football and had, in fact, played for Suffolk as an amateur. Consequently football was an important extra-curricular activity at Brynmelyn School, and being good enough to belong to the First Eleven was considered a great honour.

An excerpt from the book tells us, *"... about 1919 four brothers Verjee, Asians from a Kenya merchant family, came to Brynmelyn, and three of them played for the first football team. They and their cousin Kassam, who was very clever, used often to stay for the holidays ..."*

I am grateful to Kass Verjee for introducing Olive Hallam's book to me. Kass describes the circumstances in which he became aware of the book. He writes:

"In about September 1979 I had a phone call from someone who asked me if I was Kassam Verjee. I think I said yes and she then asked me if I had been schooled in Weston-Super-Mare. My first reaction was to say no, and then I remembered that my father had been to school there with his brother and cousins.

In conversation it transpired that the Kassam Verjee, Olive Hallam referred to was in fact Kassam Janmohamed Hasham Verjee. She was the daughter of the headmaster and she remembered Kassam particularly well as he had excelled on the playing field, and she told me that he had represented the school in the first team. I then informed her that he had died many years previously at an early age, as had my father, Rahemtulla Kassam Suleman Verjee, who was known to her as Ray. Olive Hallam told me she was writing a booklet about the school and

Picture shows Verjee cousins in Bournemouth during school holidays in August 1922. Standing second from left: Rajabali Kassam Suleman Verjee. On deck chairs, third from left: Nazerali Madatali Suleman Verjee and third from right, my father, Kassam Janmohamed Hasham Verjee. Sitting on grass, third from left: Gulamali Madatali Suleman Verjee, next to him Janu Hussein Suleman Verjee; second from right: Hassanali Hussein Suleman Verjee.

Picture shows some of the Verjee boys on a Charabanc, on holiday in Berlin in 1925. Second from the right is Hassanali Hussein Suleman Verjee, with my father in hat behind him. Next to them is Rajabali Kassam Suleman Verjee.

she wondered whether I would contribute to the cost of the book. I did contribute, and she sent me some copies of the book when it was done."

Looking back at the list of Verjee boys who were educated in England during my father's time, it is curious that only one, Bahadurali Kassam Suleman Verjee, returned with a University degree, having qualified as a Barrister. My father was admitted to Lincoln's Inn to study law, but never got to complete his studies. I have come to the conclusion that the families back home had a change of heart, and that the boys were encouraged to return to East Africa. I suspect the families now felt that the boys could be more useful in their expanding family businesses back home.

My father's passport tells a story. It shows that he sailed several times between Mombasa and the UK whilst he was a student. We know that he was at Brynmelyn College in

This picture shows the First Football Eleven, of the Brynmelyn School for Boys, in Weston-Super-Mare, Somerset, England in 1921-1922. Second from left in the back row is my father Kassam Janmohamed Hasham Verjee (he would have been sixteen then), and second from right is Gulamali Madatali Suleman Verjee, one of the several Verjee boys who were all boarders at Brynmelyn School, in Weston-Super-Mare at the same time as my father, as mentioned in earlier chapter.

Weston-Super-Mare from 1919. He sat for his Cambridge School Certificate Examination in Weston-Super-Mare in December 1923, at the age of 18, and his Cambridge School Certificate shows that he passed with Credits in five subjects, namely Religious Knowledge, English, English History, French and Mathematics.

During one of his visits to Kenya, in 1925, his parents got him married to my mother Rabhia, daughter of Hussein Suleman Damji. He would then have been 20 and my mother would have been 15. This could have been done for one of two reasons. One, to discourage him from going back to England for further studies, or perhaps, if he did return to England, so that he would then comport himself like a married gentleman - and be better equipped to resist the charms of foreign women!

Moving Between
England and Kenya

My sister Maleksultan was born in September 1926. Sadly, she died in November 1927. Roshan was born in January 1928, Sultan in October 1929, and I was born in June 1931. All of us were born in Kisumu. My grandfather, Janmohamed Hasham died in Mombasa in 1931. I am sure that my father could not have continued with his studies but for the moral support of his brothers Manji and Hussein Janmohamed. By all accounts my grandfather had left the family quite well provided for. Thus my father continued to study in England, visiting Kenya at intervals. On one occasion he brought my mother, Sultan and me to London, and we stayed in London from 1935/1937 during which time he was at Lincoln's Inn studying law, and he was also the Mukhi of London Jamat. His Kamadia was Bahadurali Kassam Suleman Verjee, himself an ex-Brynmelyn student. There was much excitement in England during that time. King George V passed away. His successor Edward VIII renounced the throne to marry the American socialite Wallis Simpson. King George VI became the King of Great Britain and Ireland.

My father's passport shows that he finally returned to Kenya in January 1939. The clouds of war were by then gathering over Europe and my father simply had to return to Kenya for good.

He must have become used to long sea voyages, for in those days, to go to England, one boarded a ship in Kilindini harbour in Mombasa. The ship would sail North, round the horn of Africa, visit Djibouti, sail through the Red Sea, through the Suez Canal, then Port Said, and into the Mediterranean Ocean. Because he mostly used to sail on ships belonging to the French company, Messagerie Maritime, the voyages would terminate in Marseilles.

The voyage took nearly three weeks. He then boarded a train to Calais, took the boat train to Dover, and then on to London.

My mother, Sultan and I also followed the same route when we went to England in 1935. We traced the same route back to Mombasa in 1937. I did the same voyage from Marseilles to Mombasa again in 1956 – this time when my first wife Munira and I were returning to Kenya after a European holiday.

The First HH Aga Khan
Education Board – Mombasa 1918

Picture shows the five members of the first HH The Aga Khan Education Board, formed in Mombasa in 1918. Sitting from left to righ: Mr Hussein Suleman Damji, Mr Maherali Valli Issa, Mr Madatali Suleman Verjee (Chairman), Mr Abdulrasul Somji, and Mr Cassam Nurmohamed. Standing behind them is their support team, consisting of Mr Hussein J Mullani, Mr Gulam Hussein, Mr Hasham Vellani & Mr Abdulla Pradhan Ladak. This event is regarded by many as the birth of modern education in Kenya.

THE AGA KHAN HIGH

Madatali Suleman Verjee was the Chairman of what must have been one of the earliest, if not the very first, Aga Khan Education Boards in Kenya. This was in 1918. The formation of the Education Board in that year was the beginning of the creation of the Aga Khan Schools network in Kenya.

I understand that Madatali's brother, Kassam Suleman Verjee, was an activist in Colonial Kenya, and was a member of the Advisory Committee set up by the British Governor to address the educational concerns of the Asian community. This had to do with the fact that Asian children had no choice but to attend British government-aided Church Mission Society schools, which were the only schools available, and where Bible studies were compulsory. The concept of multi-faith schools had not yet seen born. It became evident that non-denominational school facilities would need to be created, or schools to cater for students of different faiths. These factors were partly responsible for the sending of Asian boys, from families who could afford it, and who increasingly placed a high value on education, away from home to India or to the UK for their education. The Verjee boys' experiences are covered in the previous section, "Brynmelyn: Verjee Boys in England 1920s/30s".

By all accounts, the British government was not averse to different communities having their own schools, so long as they were funded by the communities themselves. It was in this context that Kassam Suleman Verjee, with his brothers Madatali and Hussein, donated a hundred thousand rupees towards the Aga Khan High School in Mombasa.

The first Aga Khan High School in Mombasa opened in November 1918. According to the diary of Hassanali Hussein Suleman Verjee, ".... *Kassam Suleman Verjee (with Madatali and*

Hussein) made a donation of 100,000 Rupees toward the Aga Khan School in 1916 …". The opening ceremony was performed by Sheikh Salim Bin Khalfan. It was situated on Old Kilindini Road. Eight short years later, in 1926, and having started from scratch, the school made history when a number of students passed what was then known as the Cambridge University Preliminary Overseas Examination.

And only twelve years after it opened in 1930, a new Aga Khan High School was built in Mombasa (behind the Naaz Cinema), in response to increasing demand. This was made possible by magnificent donations from Rajabali Kassam Suleman Verjee and his brothers. The school was opened on 26th of September 1930 by the then Governor of Kenya, His Excellency Sir Edward Grig. The only formal education I have had was at this school between 1937 and 1945.

The new school was qualified to teach students up to Junior Cambridge (in 1932) and then eventually the Cambridge University School Certificate Senior Overseas Examination. That was the highest level of education attainable in Kenya at the time. Between the years of 1941 and 1965, 58% of the students who sat the Senior Cambridge examination passed.

MY CLASS – THE CLASS OF '45

I myself belong to the Class of 1945. Just two boys managed a pass in the Senior Cambridge exam that year. One was Nurdin Shamsudin Tejpar, and I was the other – I was fourteen at the time. I managed to do my Senior Cambridge at the relatively early age of fourteen due to a set of fortuitous circumstances. I first joined the Aga Khan School in Mombasa when we came back from England in 1937. I was excused Primary and pre-Primary classes because their main function was to teach the English alphabet to boys who were starting to learn English, whereas I already spoke the language. (This was before the introduction of Nursery Schools). So I started at Standard One, thus saving two years. It also meant, however, that boys in my class were generally two years older - and bigger than I was.

I believe that was when I acquired the nick-name "Bhurio" which – unflatteringly - means "the white one". The name was not a reflection on my skin pigmentation. Rather, it was to do with the fact that, having lived in London for a while, I spoke English. The English language teachers at the school were all Indians, from India. They were proficient in the written language, in terms of vocabulary, grammar, syntax, and their acquaintance with English literature. Their accents however, were poor.

Having heard me speak, the Headmaster decreed that I should be taken to Senior classes to speak sentences in English, so that the boys could get a feel for how English was spoken in England. Predictably, I became the most hated boy in the Senior school at the time!

This problem of learning to speak English with a reasonable accent persisted all through my school years. I had a series of brilliant English language teachers, all Indians, who again spoke the language indifferently. We were eventually advised by our headmaster, Mr.

Badrudin Pirmohamed, that we should listen to BBC radio broadcasts if we wanted to improve our accents. In those days apparently the BBC only recruited newscasters who spoke what was known as "the King's English", and even people with regional accents could not expect to get on air.

Inevitably, due to my facility with English, I came to the notice of the school bullies, who felt I needed to be cut down to size. Two of them happened to be in my class. To spare their blushes, I will simply call them Raj and Jaff. Apart from physical intimidation, their favoured method of tormenting me was to take away my compass box, or my paint box or my pen, and only returning them to me when it was time to go home. God knows what they wanted with my compass set because they could not draw a straight line between the two of them; nor would they have recognised an isosceles triangle even if they happened to sit on the apex of one.

There was no point in complaining about them. They were both big lads, especially Raj, who was an arrogant six-footer, and I am pretty sure even the teachers treated them with a certain amount of circumspection. Raj and Jaff also enjoyed the respect of the class for they claimed to be knowledgeable about sex. For instance, they claimed they could tell if a woman had ever had a physical relationship with a man, simply by the way she walked! For a twelve year old like me this was pretty impressive stuff.

They were also responsible for the only occasion on which I got caned by the Headmaster during my school days. There were two boys (who shall remain nameless) in our school at the time, who both came from a prominent and influential family in the community. They came to the notice of Raj and Jaff because firstly, they were well behaved and decent chaps. They also differed from other boys because during recess, they ate home-made snacks rather than bhajia and chatni under the enormous Neem tree like all other normal boys. But what got the bullies going was when these two boys started coming to school in two matching Raleigh racing cycles with white plastic mudguards. The last straw for Raj and Jaff was when, thanks to their family clout, they were allowed to park these splendid bicycles in the area reserved for staff bicycles, a spot which was a strictly no-go area for other boys.

There were murmurs of discontent at this obvious favouritism. Raj and Jaff decided that the two boys had to be sorted out. They became judge and jury, and fiendishly decided that I would be the executioner. They decreed that one or both cousins needed to be beaten up, and that I would be the person to do it. I told them that I could not do it. I had never hit anybody in my life, and what is more, I was afraid, for I have never been the physical type. Raj gave me a stark choice. Either I would do what they wanted, or else they would beat me up first and then have a go at the two boys. They assured me that I had nothing to fear because they would be standing right behind me when I hit the boy.

On the appointed day, we lurked outside the school fence by the rear entrance, waiting for the boy to come out of school on his fancy bicycle. He dismounted when he saw us blocking his path. The gang started chanting "Hit him, hit him." I had never struck anyone before and I did not know what to do, so I simply pushed him. He was not expecting this sudden lunge from me and he fell quite badly, I think. He was more shocked than hurt, but he managed to pick himself up, with tears in his eyes, did not say anything, and simply took his bike and trundled it away.

A satisfied Raj then explained his philosophy to all present. He said these "sons of rich men" had no spine and would never retaliate. We should never be afraid of them. We had just seen one of them slink away without a word!

The next morning, during the first period, which was always English Language, the Headmaster's clerk appeared with a note and handed it to Mr. Muljani, the English teacher. I was being summoned to the Headmaster's office. I entered this inner sanctum with foreboding. The Headmaster, Mr. Gulamali Alibhai, looked even sterner than usual. Across his desk sat the father of the boy whom I had pushed off his bike on the previous day. "Did you and a gang of boys attack Mr. MDL's son yesterday?" I started to stutter an explanation but I could not formulate a sentence. "Did you or did you not?" I responded, "Yes Sir, but …." He said he did not want any explanations and that he would not tolerate hooliganism from his students. And then he asked me what I thought was an amazingly irrelevant question under the circumstances, "Which hand do you write with?"

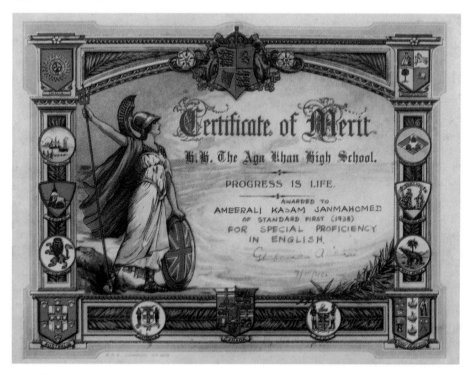

Certificate for Special Proficiency in English awarded in 1938 and signed by the Headmaster, Mr Gulamali Alibhai.

"Right hand, Sir." I said. Then he stood up and asked me to stretch out my left hand with palm facing upwards. He picked up one of the several canes which seemed to grow out of his waste paper basket like branches of a malevolent tree and administered two deliberate lashes on the palm of my left hand. Then I heard him say "You can go now." Tears in my eyes prevented me from seeing the expression on Mr. MDL's face as I left. Was honour satisfied? I don't know what hurt more. Was it the physical pain, or was it hurt pride and humiliation, or was it the feeling of injustice? Perhaps a little bit of everything.

(Some twenty years later, I was appointed to the Ismaili Provincial Council in Mombasa, and sitting on my left was none other than Mr. MDL himself who was also a member of the Council. He gave no sign, even if he did remember that episode. Both he and his son got along very well with me in latter years. I don't know what happened to Raj, for one day he was gone, never to be seen again. I met Jaff twenty-five years later when I was the President of the Council. I had started a regular weekly Surgery where people with problems could ask us for assistance. He had come for help for he was in some serious trouble. We were able to help him).

I managed to get promoted at that school each year until 1943, when I failed my Kenya Preliminary exam ignominiously. Whilst I had done well in all other subjects, I had failed abysmally in the compulsory subject of Mathematics, which consisted of Arithmetic, Algebra and Geometry.

The following year the Head Master of the School, Mr. Gulamali Alibhai, retired after years of distinguished service. He was succeeded by a Mr. Badrudin Pirmohamed. Mr. Pirmohamed was a new generation educationalist who wanted to introduce new systems into the school. He felt however that the transition would be greatly facilitated if the school could get rid of the older boys first. I seem to remember that there were a number of older boys who appeared to be languishing in the Junior, Sub-Senior and Senior Classes at that time. With the blessings of the Education Board, Mr. Pirmohamed came up with the idea that he would create a new Senior class which would include all the boys from these three classes, plus the failed boys from the Kenya Preliminary exam, and give them the opportunity to sit the Senior Cambridge Exam after two years - that is, in 1945! Fail or pass, however, he would expect all participants in this experiment to leave the school at the end of 1945.

For me, this seemed like a short cut to success. My father did not think it was such a clever idea for a twelve year old, who had just failed his Kenya Preliminary exam, to attempt Senior Cambridge in just two years. However, thanks to some judicious threats of a hunger strike and intercession on my behalf from my mother, my father relented and allowed me to enrol in this new Senior Class.

The Assembly Hall on the first floor became our class room. We started the year with some forty boys. There was considerable disparity between the ages of students in this class.

There were pretty senior boys like Shahbudin Nurmohamed Dossa, Rajabali KS Damji and several others on one hand, and on the other hand, there I was – just twelve years old. I also seem to remember two non-Ismaili boys in that class. They were Yusufali Taherali Patwa and Yusufali Dar. I remember them as studious and extremely well behaved boys.

Aga Khan High School boy scouts leaders 1944. Sitting from left to right: Myself as the Hon Sec of the Court of Honour, Mohamedali Mohan Amarshi, Zulfiqar Abdulrasul Dhalla, Shamsu Meghji – Asst Scout Master, Mohamedali Nurmohamed – Scout Master, Amir HS Meghji – Troop Leader, Umedali Gokal Ladha. Sadru Abdulla Alibhai Kanji & Amir Abdulrasul Dhala. Standing from left to right: Rajabali Nanji, Kassamali Karachiwalla, Pyarali Hassan Juma, Tajdin Jivan Kanji and Ramzan Ahmed Jamal.

And – twenty years later, at Imamat Day celebrations in Mombasa, Mukhi Ameer Janmohamed, Major Shamsu Gilani, Girl Guides Leader Shirin Habib Alibhai, Scout Master Mohamedali Hasham Nurmohamed and Ladies Volunteers Captain MA Kulsum.

MY TEACHERS

I remember our teachers. Mr. Pirmohamed and Mr. Muljani taught us English Language, English Literature and Geography. Mr. Shah taught us Gujarati. Mr. Narshi Patel was our Mathematics teacher. Mr. Bhimani taught us British History, also Hygiene and Physiology. My saviour was Mr. Shukla, our Arts teacher. I call him my saviour because Senior Cambridge gave me the choice of either Arts or Mathematics, which had been my nemesis in my previous examination. He taught me enough about object drawing, and perspectives and so on to enable me to pass in Arts.

I would specially like to mention Mr. Mohamedali Hasham Nurmohamed. He was our Religion teacher as well as the Scout Master. His uncle Cassam Nurmohamed was one of the original Education Board members of 1918.

Mohamedali Master will long be remembered by hundreds, perhaps several thousand Ismaili boys who studied at The Aga Khan High in Mombasa during that period. It was he who taught us Ismaili History. I shall always be indebted to him for teaching me our Ginans, their traditional ragas, and their meanings.

(Reciting Ginans in different Jamat Khanas of the world has now become a passion of mine. Although I had learnt Ginans at an early age, I did not have the courage to recite them in public. I recited my first Ginan in public at Putney Jamat Khana in 1999, when the then Mukhi Azim Jivraj and Kamadia Riaz Jamal really pushed and encouraged me to do so. Since then, I have been privileged to recite Ginans in thirty-four Jamat Khanas in eleven different countries of the world, from Melbourne and Sydney in the East, to Lions Gate Jamat Khana in Vancouver, in the West. The greatest experience of all for me was reciting a Ginan in Karachi's Garden Jamat Khana [the largest Ismaili Jamat Khana in the world] with some two thousand plus voices joining in).

Both my sisters Roshan and Sultan also sat the Senior Cambridge examination in 1945, as students of the White Sisters' Convent School. They each managed a Second Grade Pass, whereas I only secured a Third Grade Pass.

Eventually, the old building behind the Naaz Cinema became the Kenya Secondary School, KENSEC, which has now merged with the Aga Khan Academy situated on the sea-front in Lighthouse.

The 1918 Photocall
Links with Past and Present

I would like to go back to the 1918 photograph of the Aga Khan Education Board, because I can trace relationships, or connections with, most of the people in the picture.

Hussein Suleman Damji, sitting first on the left, was my maternal grandfather. He had four sons, and two daughters, Rabhia who was my mother, and Fatma, who got married to Janmohamed (Janu), son of Cassam Nurmohamed, sitting on the extreme right.

This union between the son and daughter of the two members of the Education Board has produced some talented academics, three of whom are Professors in Universities in Britain and the U.S. All three are great grandsons of the two Board members and grandchildren of Janmohamed Cassam and his wife Fatma.

SHIRAZ DOSSA, is the son of Mr. Abdul Nurmohamed Dossa and Sultan, daughter of Janu Massa and Fatma Massi. He did his BA (Hons) at Makerere University in Uganda, MA in Political Science and PhD in Political Theory at the University of Toronto. He is Professor of Political Science at St. Francis Xavier University in Nova Scotia and Adjunct Professor, Faculty of Graduate Studies, Department of Political Studies at Dalhousie University, Halifax, Nova Scotia. He has been the recipient of numerous Honours and Awards from University of Helsinki, University of British Columbia, and University of Calgary.

QUASSIM CASSAM is the son of Amir Janmohamed Cassam and my sister Sultan, grandson of Janu Massa and Fatma Massi. He was born in Mombasa, educated at Mill Hill and Oxford. Zeenat and I attended his Degree Ceremony at the Sheldonian Theatre in Oxford in January 1986. It was an amazing event, even for Oxford University. He was the recipient of four Degrees on that same day. They were a BA, an MA, a B Phil and a D Phil in Philosophy.

Quassim was then elected to an Official Fellowship in Philosophy at Wadham College, Oxford. He was Visiting Associate Professor at the University of California, Berkeley and also held the John Evans Distinguished Visiting Professorship in Moral and Intellectual Philosophy at Northwestern University, Illinois, USA. He left Oxford to become Professor of Philosophy at University College London in 2005. He accepted the Knightbridge Chair at Cambridge University in 2007. His disciplines include metaphysics, epistemology, philosophy of mind, modern philosophy and Kant.The author of two published works, "Self and World", and "The Possibility of Knowledge", he is also the Editor of the Oxford publication, "Self-Knowledge".

MAHMOUD SHIVJI is the son of Sadru Hirji Shivji and Gulshan, daughter of Janu Massa and Fatma Massi. Dr. Shivji is a Professor at the Nova South Eastern University Oceanographic Center and Director, Guy Harvey Research Institute. His specialisation is in Genetics, Molecular Marine Biology and Biology of Sharks. Dr. Shivji and his Associates made world head-lines recently when they reported the Virgin birth of a hammerhead shark under laboratory conditions.

One of Cassam Nurmohamed's daughters, Sambai, got married to Hasham Vellani, standing second from the right. Their grand-daughter Zeiny is married to Bahadur Hirji. Zeenat and I list them among our very dear friends.

Second from left, Mr Maherali Vali Essa served as the Kamadia when my grandfather Janmohamed Hasham was the Mukhi of the Kuze Jamat Khana in Mombasa between 1925 and 1927.

Next to him is Madatali Suleman Verjee, Chairman of the Board, whose family's major donation enabled the new Aga Khan School to be built in 1930. His sons Nazerali and Gulamali were at Brynmelyn College at the same time as my father in the early 1920s. Gulamali Kaka also played in the College Football First Eleven. Nazerali Kaka was a wicket-keeper in the cricket eleven.

Seated second from right is Mr Abdulrasul Somji. Zeenat and I count his two grand-sons, Dr Shamsudin (Miller) Somji and Ameer Somji, and their wives, Gulis both, as our dearest friends. Ameer and I used to be tennis partners and on one famous occasion reached the finals of the Coast Open Junior Tennis Championships in Mombasa. We lost to one Yusuf Karim and his partner. Yusuf Karim, of course, went on to become the Coast Senior Champion.

Miller and Ameer Somji both studied at the Aga Khan High. Miller went on to become a Doctor and Ameer joined his family business. We were also among the original Directors of Diamond Trust of Kenya when the Company went public in 1972. Ameer and I became business partners in London in 1975. We have had a most enjoyable, and successful, relationship and are more like brothers than anything else.

Photo shows Ameer Somji and myself outside the entrance to the Oatlands Park Hotel, Weybridge, Surrey.

Since I left the Aga Khan High School in 1945, I have been privileged to have been the Chairman of the Old Boys Association (before political correctness made it necessary to call it the Former Students Association). I have also served as a member of the Aga Khan Education Board. The memory I cherish most is of the occasion in 1963, when as a Rotarian, I was responsible for forming the First Inter-Act Club on the African Continent with its home in my Alma Mater, The Aga Khan High School of Mombasa.

The object of Inter-act is to introduce the concept of Community and International service to boys and girls of between 14 to 18. They are sponsored by Rotary Clubs, but are self-governing.

The successor to that school which opened in Old Kilindini Road in 1918 is of course the Aga Khan Academy, which opened in December 2003 on the Mombasa sea-front. One hopes that boys and girls who study there will appreciate that they are beneficiaries of a school system which goes back to 1918. Not a bad memorial to the five Education Board Members whose photo appears at the beginning of this chapter. It is pleasing to know that the Aga Khan Schools are well and thriving in the new millennium.

The first Community Service project of the Interact Club of the Aga Khan High School was to rebuild the steps to the Missions to Seamen club in Mombasa. Picture shows club members on site with Rotary committee members Aziz Kassim-Lakha, Yusuf Mamujee and me.

"The Cold Within"

"The Cold Within"

A favoured English poem of mine is entitled "The Cold Within". Sadly the author is not known. I came across it in a Christian magazine, "The Watchtower" I believe - in the nineteen-fifties, and it has stayed in my mind, for to me this poem spells out eloquently those things which divide human beings – divisions created by nature and further exacerbated by humans themselves. God may have created man in his own image; all men may have been created equal; we may all be descendants of Noah and Adam and Eve. God gave man intellect and man deployed it, amongst other things, in the pursuit of discovering and creating imaginative ways in which man would differ from man. These diversities are often explained away by claiming that these differences are Divine Will. He created us with different colours, tongues, ethnicities, so that we could get to know one another and be introduced to our different ways, which make the family of Adam and Eve more interesting. But could the same goal not have been achieved without making people in different colours?

For me, this poem says it so well. It is a story of six human beings, who find themselves marooned, out of doors, on a dark and bitterly cold, freezing night. They sit huddled around a log fire. The only way in which they can survive through the night is if they keep the fire going till daybreak. But the fire is about to die, for it is running out of logs.

And yet, the fire does not need to die, for each one of the humans is holding a piece of wood in his hands, and all they need to do is to keep feeding the fire, one at a time, and it would see them through the night until the warmth of the morning sun comes out.

"The Cold Within"

Six humans, trapped by happenstance,
In dark and bitter cold;
Each one holding a piece of wood,
As the story is told.

Their dying fire, in need of logs;
The first woman held hers back.
For on the faces around the fire,
She noticed one was black.

The next man looking across the way,
Sees one not of his church;
He could not bring himself to give the fire,
His stick of birch.

The third man sat in tattered clothes.
He gave his coat a hitch;
Why should my log be put to use,
To warm the idle rich?

The rich man sat back and thought
Of all the wealth he had in store,
And how to keep all he had collected,
From the lazy, shiftless poor.

The black man's face bespoke revenge,
Whilst the fire died in the night.
For all he could see in his piece of wood was a chance;
A chance to spite the white.

The last man of this forlorn group,
Did nothing except for gain;
Giving only to those who gave,
That is how he played his game.

So now we have one dead fire and six dead bodies,
Each one still clutching his piece of wood - proof of human sin.
They did not die of the cold without.
These people - they died from the cold within.

AFRICA IN MY TIME

The African continent was historically the subject of a scramble for colonies by European powers, and the political map of the continent at the end of the First World War shows that Britain, France, Portugal, Germany, Belgium, Spain and Italy had neatly divided up the continent between them. The Europeans brought along their religious, cultural, political and economic agendas with them to the virgin continent which was Africa. In the minds of some Europeans, Africa was also a source of obtaining slaves for the now prosperous slave trade. Civilising the natives and saving their souls was the ostensible reason. The concept of introducing democracy was an afterthought. In any event, how does one democratise the unenfranchised?

Britain probably owned more real estate in Africa than other countries. And the three East African territories of Kenya, Uganda and Tanganyika were part of the vast British Empire. I believe that the British rule was benign in comparison with that of other European powers. It has also been said that the British may have been arrogant and patronising, but they provided good governance.

Born in Kenya in 1931, I lived there during my childhood except for a couple of years when I was in London with my parents between 1935 and 1937. In my childish innocence I was blissfully oblivious of racial considerations. Whilst I was living through it, my own protected existence did not expose me to the realities of racial discrimination. I had not cottoned on to the fact that there was a pecking order in colonial Kenya, with Europeans being on top, Asians, mainly Indians, in the lower middle, and the Africans at the bottom of the pile. I had never wondered why there were no Europeans and Africans in my school. I had never wondered why the hospitals I went to also had no African or European patients. In my childish innocence I had accepted all this as the natural order of things. Inevitably, as I grew older, I became increasingly aware of Kenya's racial structure, and I began to come face to face with its ramifications.

We used to live in a rented apartment in Mombasa. I was aware that my family owned several prestige properties. One of them was the City House, which had a number of shops, offices and desirable apartments. I asked my father - my father, who had been educated in England for so many years - who was a Charter Member of the Mombasa Rotary Club - who was a Municipal Councillor – why we did not live in our own property. He said that although we owned the property, all our tenants were Europeans and it would not be such a good idea for us to move into the City House apartments.

My father died in 1950 and I replaced him as a Director of City House. Soon after, I learnt that an apartment was going to be available shortly, and I informed my Company that I was moving in. A week after Munira and I moved in, our European neighbour across the landing gave notice of vacating his apartment immediately. Within a matter of two months all the other European tenants were also gone. I began to understand what my father had been trying to explain to me without spelling it out in so many words. However, there is a happy ending to this story. Given that our apartments were desirable and were in a prime location, we were able to re-let them at once, and at better rents than before. And all new tenants knew that this particular block of apartments was not exclusively for any one race, and that, in fact, an Asian family already occupied one of the apartments. Our new tenants were a mixed bag of Europeans and Asians, but as yet, no Africans.

THE CLUBS

Different races, even communities, led insulated lives, with their own churches, both Catholic and Anglican, Mandirs, Masjids and Jamat Khanas, their own schools, they were apart even in death for they had their own cemeteries, only mingling with others when they had to. And they all had their own clubs. The Europeans had their Mombasa Club, and the Mombasa Sports Club, the Mombasa Golf Club and the Yacht Club. And the Indians had the Aga Khan Club, the Goan Institute, the Patel Samaj, the Bohra Club, the Ithna-Ashri Club and the Navnat Vanik Mahajan. The Indian Sports Club was an exception, where any upper crust Indian could belong provided he satisfied the election criteria. There was no club for Africans.

My business, Badrudin's Sports House, used to supply sports equipment to most clubs on the island. Amongst them we used to supply golf balls to the Mombasa Golf Club on the sea front. Usually, our man Musyoka would deliver them on his bicycle. I remember the occasion when he was not available and I undertook to drop them off myself. I parked my car in the car park and walked into the club house, looking for someone to accept the balls and sign for them. European establishments in those days had African stewards and waiters who wore starched white uniforms, who padded around the polished wooden floors on white tennis shoes, and were well-versed in the ways of the white man. Many long serving members of the staff also acquired the haughtiness befitting a club where only European members could use the club's facilities. This race thing had rubbed off on these lackeys.

On this occasion I was accosted by one of these supercilious types and he asked me what I was doing inside the Club premises. I told him I was looking for somebody to take delivery of golf balls which had been ordered. He told me I was not allowed to enter the Club premises through the front, that there was a Service entrance on the side of the Club house for deliveries. He warned me never to enter the club house itself in future, and to remove my car at once from what was strictly the Members car park.

Whilst hotels had to open their doors to all, white man's clubs held out until the very last, even after independence was achieved by countries from their former rulers. You could still see vestiges of the "attitude," whether you went to the "Chhini" Club in Mombasa, or the Sindh Club in Karachi, or the Yacht Club in Kisumu, or the CCI in Bombay. These clubs sheltered behind their "constitutions," where membership proposals or applications could be 'black-balled' by anonymous objectors. I think it was George Orwell who described the English male's Sports and Social Club as "his spiritual home – a hallowed institution; where they had sanctuaries, like the Men's Bar and the Snooker room, where they could even seek refuge from the females of the species".

I distinctly remember the Mombasa Sports Club. A strictly Europeans-only club. It had the best manicured cricket field on the island and it seemed as if even the grass grew respectfully on their Rugby ground. Their pitches had no brown patches of dirt such as you could find on all other grounds in Mombasa. The stones which marked out the boundary of the cricket field were always evenly spaced. They shone in the Kenya sun because they had been chalked white. This club also had the only team on the island that wore boots when they played football.

THE EMPIRE DAY

There was, however, one day each year during my school days, when everybody was allowed to go to the Mombasa Sports Club. It was on 24th May each year. It was known as Empire Day. Students of every school turned out in their best uniforms and marched to the Mombasa Sports Club, each one carrying a small Union Jack stapled to a stick. We were all actually allowed to stand on the hallowed turf of the Rugby ground. There were many hundreds of boys and girls from different schools in the Coast Province. We all stood at attention. At the appointed time, Provincial Commissioner Coast would turn up in the official Humber Super Snipe, resplendent in an immaculate white starched uniform, with a white plumed helmet, and a ceremonial sword at his side. He would mount the little dais which had been put up for the occasion, and the band would strike up the National Anthem. We had all been taught the words and we wished King George VI to long reign over us. The PC would then make a loyal speech which could be heard for miles thanks to the public address system, only occasionally distorted when a gust of cool wind blew in from the Indian Ocean. He reminded the assembled boys and girls of how privileged we all were to belong to this happy family, this Empire.

One nice thing about Empire Day, apart from the fact that there was no school on the day, was that each boy and girl who attended the annual Empire Day parade was given a china mug with a crossed Union Jack design with the portrait of King George VI embossed on it.

A Voyage to London in 1948

I suppose volumes could be filled with anecdotes of racial experiences of people during those days. I give below the experiences of my good friend (and Bridge companion) Tajdin Mohamedali Dhala. Taj, along with two other good friends of mine, Mohamed Jaffer Ismail Jaffer, and Sadruddin Abdulla Alibhai Kanji, was off to the UK for further studies in August 1948. Taj writes as follows:

"…but the greatest shock to me was when I boarded the ship S.S. Modassa on 17th August 1948 (from Mombasa) at the age of 17, for a sea voyage to Britain for further education…Most passengers were British farmers and government civil servants who had not visited their relatives in Britain for several years.

Altogether there were eighty young Asians who had waited for the war to be over and catch the first transport available to get to various British Universities. At home we had all followed the curriculum set by Cambridge University, so it was natural that we wanted to go to Britain for further education. We also regarded Britain at the pinnacle of the British Empire, with London as its hub.

So the 8000 ton Modassa, with 450 passengers, set sail north from the equator at a steady speed of eight nautical miles. The captain had charted his ship to sail to south western coast of Saudi Arabia, to call at Aden to enter the Red Sea, pass through Suez Canal and into the Mediterranean. Then west to Straits of Gibraltar, Bay of Biscay and dock at Plymouth. The voyage was to take 21 days.

We had a last look at the shores of Kenya and settled down in our bunks in the lower deck…cabins on the upper decks were for white passengers only. We had no other choice as the only other passenger ships which sailed to London from Mombasa were the Union Castle Line ships. They would not accept Asian passenger because of their links with South Africa.

The ship's Purser had put up a notice for meal times. All Asian passengers had to take their dinner quickly at a much earlier time as the dining room could not accommodate all passengers at the same time'…we soon realised that this was so that the Europeans could then be served a leisurely dinner at a more appropriate time…to us it seemed blatant discrimination. We had paid the same fares and why this treatment?

A few students discussed this issue and set up a committee to talk to the Purser to see if any change could be made to our meal times. He would not, so a delegation was formed to have a word with the Captain. His immediate retort was "This is my ship and I am the Commander. Either you do as you are told or I will order you off the ship at the next port of call, which is Aden."

Taj concludes by stating,

"This episode left a bitter taste and I wondered whether I would face the same situation when I landed in Plymouth. During my stay in London for the next four years I had the most wonderful relationships with a number of English families and made many friends. I did not encounter any apparent racial discrimination."

The two pictures above include Sadru Abdullah Alibhai Kanji, Umed Ladha, myself, Talib Ahmed, Taj Dhalla, Jimmy Damji and Mohamed Jaffar, Tajdin Esmail Mawji (Tailo) crowching in front.

Discrimination was still in evidence even after Kenya's independence in 1963. Hitherto whites-only boarding schools had to open their doors to students of all races. The facilities and the standard of education were vastly superior to those of other schools in the country. Parents of African and Asian children were keen to get their sons and daughters enrolled.

But coloured boys had to undergo a baptism of fire before they would be allowed to settle in. Bullying had always been an accepted feature in English public schools, and the senior boys now had a whole underclass of coloured boys to bully and to abuse as '"fags". Indian boys suffered most. Generally, African students were sons of powerful officials or politicians – they were also quite physical – and white students and the school staff were soon made to realise that they were not to be trifled with. On the other hand, Indian boys were fair game. They were mostly puny, and though sons of wealthy parents they had no political clout and their wealth cut no ice in the school environment. There was also an affinity between white boys and the Africans which the Indians did not share. All of them were Christians, practicing or otherwise, and even more significantly, they would eat whatever was placed in front of them. Indian students on the other hand, had special cultural requirements and diets. There were not only Hindus and Muslims, many of them also belonged to different sects within those religions. Most of them did not eat pork and many were vegetarians.

THE TRAIN JOURNEY BETWEEN NAIROBI AND MOMBASA

In my view, the train journey between Mombasa and Nairobi epitomised the way in which the three main racial groups lived in Kenya.

Kenya Uganda Railways used to run a daily passenger train service between Mombasa and Nairobi. The Mombasa train would leave each evening at six pm to arrive at Nairobi at 8.00 a.m. the following morning. The Nairobi train would leave at seven to arrive at Mombasa at 8.00 am the next morning. Nairobi being at an altitude of 5500 feet above sea level, the journey down to the coast took an hour less. Each train would consist of the locomotive and tender and several goods vans. The carriages were arranged in a specific manner. Behind the locomotive would be a number of Third Class carriages, followed by a couple of Second Class carriages, and then some First Class carriages, with the Restaurant Car in the middle. Then some more Second Class carriages, some goods vans and the Guards van bringing up the rear. The reason for this was that in the days of the coal-burning locomotives, there used to be a lot of soot in the front half of the train. This way, the Europeans were spared the soot and also did not have to walk too far to reach the Restaurant car. Somewhere along the line, the coal burning-locomotives were replaced by Garratt diesel locomotives, and soot was no longer a problem. The locomotives were usually named after local mountains, eg, Mount Kinangop and Mount Elgin, and so on.

Europeans travelled first class. Cabins were better appointed and cost more. The Europeans ordered from bar service before going in for dinner, and had a choice of two sittings. A smartly turned out waiter in a starched white tunic with brass buttons would announce the sittings by walking through the carriages playing a tune on a shiny xylophone. The restaurant

Steward was usually a Goan and the waiters Africans, well trained. The food was good, with a four course meal consisting of soup, a fish course, meat and veg and dessert, with coffee and liqueurs to follow. First class cabins would be turned down whilst the passengers were at dinner, with crisp white bedding which would have been pre-ordered. Most Europeans also went in for breakfast in the morning.

Indians mostly travelled second class. The carriages were less sumptuously appointed, or were old first class carriages. Indians did not as a rule go to the Restaurant car. They brought their own cooked food in "tiffins" which they ate in their cabins. The menu for our family usually consisted of fried fish and "rotli" or "rotlo". For Roshan, Sultan and I, that meal was the highlight of the journey. Indians also travelled with their own bed-rolls. Indians in those days did not stay in hotels, so they always stayed with families and friends, and they always carried their own bedding. In any case, there were no hotels which catered for them, even if any Indian wanted to stay in one. I don't think staying in hotels fitted in with the Indian culture. Well-to-do Indians always had relatives - cousins, or in-laws, or friends or business connections, who would be happy to put up out of town visitors. Poorer people would find guest-houses, known as Dharamshalas or Musafar-Khanas which were usually run by community groups.

We used to make this trip each year during school holidays and would stay in Nairobi at our Ebrahim Mama's house. One of my loveliest memories is of Roshan, Sultan and I, and our lovely cousins, all having so much fun when all the beddings were rolled out on the sitting room carpet each evening. Our cousins would refuse to go to their own beds because they wanted to be with us on the mattresses on the sitting room carpet - Nurbanu Mami and my mother would eventually succeed in shooing them away.

There was also another significant difference between the carriages in the three classes. The toilets. They were situated at each end of the carriages. First Class would have the upright Western-style toilets at both ends. Second Class had one Western and one squatting style at either end and Third Class had squatting-type toilets at both ends. You would be lucky to find any toilet paper in the Second, and certainly not in the Third. Cabins with en suite toilets and a wash-basin were introduced later.

Most Africans and some Indians travelled third class. Third class carriages were not sectioned off into cabins. They had hard wooden benches, and passengers sat through the night until they reached the destination. They paid very little for the privilege.

The trains would make a number of stops along the way when third class passengers could stretch their legs and buy mugs of tea and snacks from local vendors who came up to the carriages. From Mombasa, the first stop would be Voi, a hundred miles due West. Then Mtito-Endei which was the half way mark, and for us, Kibwezi, about two thirds of the way to Nairobi. We used to keep awake for Kibwezi because one of my cousins, Hussein Motabapa's eldest daughter Dolu, lived there – she was married to Akbar Gangji who had a business there – and they would always meet the train with lovely Indian tea and some delicious snacks at four in the morning! They would have received a telegram that family members were travelling on that day.

SETTLING IN A NEW COUNTRY

I cannot escape the feeling that the Indian community in East Africa in the early days were not too uncomfortable with the segregated life style in the Colonies. The priority for Indians was to make a decent life for themselves and their families. Many of them, including my family, succeeded beyond their wildest dreams. Furthermore, they could employ numerous servants. In our household I remember there being a number of cleaners, cook, child-minders, drivers, dhobi, gardeners and so on.

My grandfather and his peers did not seek social contacts with the Europeans and the Africans. They would only have dealt with the Europeans in so far as it was necessary. I am convinced that they were more than a little happy that the segregation which kept them apart from the Europeans, also enabled them to live in their own private little worlds, where businesses were good, they had servants, they were allowed to practice their religions as they wished, and several communities had of course created their own schools, dispensaries, clubs, libraries, cemeteries and so on. They felt safe that their women and their children were not exposed to potentially corrupt influences of other communities, and they could continue to preserve their customs and traditions. They also enjoyed the security of a Police Force which was officered by British expatriates.

Indians themselves, for centuries, had lived within the framework of the Caste system. The Caste system, though generally identified with Hinduism was also very much a part of life for the Muslim and Christian Indians who lived harmoniously with the Hindu majority in India. I believe that the Caste system is based on the premise that one is born a Brahmin (Priest and Scholarly class); or a Kshatriya (warrior class); or a Vaishya (trader); or a Shudra (service providers and artisans) - depending on what one has done in a previous incarnation. And there was yet another under-class, consisting of the Achhoots and the Bhangis (untouchables) and the Chamars and the Dhobis, who cleaned toilets and did menial works. They were not allowed to worship in the same temples. Members of higher casts would actually have to undergo a purification process if they accidentally came in physical contact with an Achhoot.

The Britishers who came to India had no difficulty in adjusting to this environment. They too came from a society which was stratified by a class system. They too had their landowning classes, their soldier classes, their priesthood, their lowly shopkeepers, and their menials, their factory workers and so on. They understood the principle of people being kept in their proper places. It also fitted in with their Victorian upper middle class stiff upper lip ethos of "dressing up for dinner in the far reaches of the Empire to keep up appearances for the benefit of the natives". So, by and large, the British found it helpful to perpetuate and even codify this inequity, for it simplified the hierarchy on which Victorian Britons thrived.

The caste system is of course now made illegal in the Indian Constitution. That is not to say that it has disappeared. Prejudices cannot be legislated away. There is considerable evidence in India – and even Pakistan – that it still features in people's thinking in numerous situations even today.

THE COLONIAL ADMINISTRATION

Each British colony had a Governor who represented the King. The country would be divided into Provinces, each with its own Provincial Commissioner. Mombasa, being in the Coast Province, would be under the authority of the PC for the Coast. The Province would be divided into Districts, each one with its own District Commissioner, and the more remote regions would be administered by a cadre of District Officers. Then there was the Judiciary and the court system. Then there would be the all-important Police Commissioners and Inspectors, and a whole spectrum of important people like the Fire Masters, and the Port Manager, and the Medical officers and Public Works and so on. All these people would be Britishers.

As Hassanali Kaka describes in his diary, Nairobi in the Year 1900, *"The colonial British government had appointed a number of officers to run the affairs of the rapidly expanding town, including a Commissioner for Native Affairs, Mr. Ainsworth, who worked alongside a European doctor, an Indian compounder, two Goan clerks, a European police inspector and a few trained African police officers. Most of the local inhabitants were Kikuyus..."*

The Sultan of Zanzibar was represented in Mombasa by a Liwali, a somewhat ceremonial appointment. The incumbent in my time was Sheikh Mbarak Ali Hinawy. He was an impressive man of considerable refinement. He would preside over a Baraza, which was a kind of court which was held each year to celebrate the occasion of Eid-ul-Fitr at the end of the holy month of Ramadan. The town's leading citizens of all races would be invited, and the top echelon of the British Government would always make it a point to attend in a show of solidarity and as a mark of respect to the large Arab, African and Indian Muslim population of the Coast Province. The end of Ramadan would have been announced on the previous day by the firing of an old Portuguese cannon outside Fort Jesus. This custom was discontinued when an English Ordnance Officer discovered that the cannon was now in a dangerous state and might explode if gunpowder was introduced into its firing mechanism.

I cannot imagine my grandfather and his friends wanting to go to European Clubs and hotels. Nor would they want their women and children to be exposed to alien influences. As stated previously, they only dealt with the Europeans when necessary. Whilst the whites were admired and respected as providers and enforcers of law and order in the country, my forefathers would not have approved of their mores. I have the impression that the Indian community jealously guarded their own traditions, their concept of racial purity, their religious sects and their social fabric.

The first challenge to face the Indians would have been to whittle down the barriers which separated one Indian community from another. Living on a new continent and facing common challenges engendered the understanding that they had to learn to live as one if they were to survive in what was a challenging, and even hostile environment. There are heart-warming stories of how Indians began to help each other in the new environment. Helping new immigrants from India, opening their doors, offering food and shelter to new arrivals, helping with advice and practical help in setting up new businesses, helping each other in times of trouble, sharing of information – all this became increasingly common. Two things remained sacrosanct however. One did not marry outside one's own community. And you worshipped your own Deity.

I don't think the Indian community treated Africans in a particularly enlightened manner. The Africans of the time were poor and uneducated. Christian missionaries started Mission schools which educated Africans and at the same time introduced them to Christianity. I don't think that Hindus and Indian Muslims were interested in either converting the Africans to their faiths, or to educate them. They only saw in the Africans a supply of servants who had to be shown how to do domestic chores – and this knowledge was always imparted by the women of the house. Judging by what I remember of our own families, I believe that over a period of time, the African house-servant and the Ayah became indispensable and integral parts of the family. In our household certainly, I seem to remember that we had a number of trusted servants who used to work in our homes for years and years. I can remember three, Abhong who was a Luo, then Sanghoro who was a Maragoli and lastly Karissa who was from the Coast. These three were trusted retainers of the family, and Abhong and Sanghoro particularly, wielded much authority over us when Roshan, Sultan and I were children.

But the upstairs-downstairs distinction was always there, and it was graphically clear: the employer was always Indian; and the servant always African. On balance however, I would suggest that the Indian was closer to the African than the European. Certainly more Indians spoke Swahili than they did English. We did not have to go to school to learn Swahili. The first words some children would have spoken would have been in Swahili rather than in Gujarati. Indeed, a number of Indians, particularly Ismailis who had lived in Zanzibar, were more at home in Swahili than Gujarati or English. Many of them who are now settled in different western countries still lapse into lilting Swahili when the mood strikes them. I myself have no opportunity to speak Swahili in London, but it comes rushing back to me as soon as I set foot on Kenyan soil.

It has been said that Indians of the time were too pre-occupied with their own challenges and problems to even recognise and acknowledge the plight of the Africans, who were even worse off than them and were discriminated against by both the Europeans and the Indians alike.

The picture shows Abhong looking after me when I was a few monthes old.

THE POLITICAL AWAKENING

By this time too, the Indian community had also became aware of the first public expressions of dissatisfaction with the British Raj in their mother country, and of the fact that people had begun to speak up, with the phrase "Quit India" gaining currency in the Indian political vocabulary.

Once again, I quote from the diary of Hassanali Hussein Suleman Verjee:

> *"In 1917 Asians living in East Africa had demanded the right to form an Indian Congress (inspired by the political movement in India). Once this was approved, Hussein Suleman Verjee was elected as the first President of the East African Indian National Congress. Delegates from Uganda and Tanganyika also attended the inaugural session of the Congress.*

> *The then Governor of Kenya, Major General Sir Edward Northey, was an invited guest and sat on the stage next to Hussein's wife Fatmabai. There must have been tension in the air, for Hussein Suleman Verjee, in his inaugural speech, openly criticised the colonial regime for its policy of social injustice and racial segregation.*

> *He talked about the fact that the Asians in Kenya had initiated trade throughout the colony by settling in remote and inhospitable areas and often facing severe hardships; lack of water, insufficient food, inadequate or non-existent medical supplies. Having contributed so much to the development of the country they were then being subjected to discriminatory policies which expropriated African land for the exclusive use of the white farmers, and refused equal rights in every significant field, including education, to both Africans and Asians.*

[It is interesting to note that the propriety of expropriating land from the Africans is not questioned, whilst the unfair apportionment of the spoils is at issue. AJ]

We are suffering from segregation. In the Highlands all the good agricultural land is reserved for the whites. The good residential and trading areas in all the major towns of this country are reserved for white men. British Indians (from British India) are not allowed in hotels and restaurants, not even in the railway dining car, but the white man's dog is allowed.

Our individual leaders' voices had fallen on deaf ears of the government. It became absolutely necessary to form the East African National Congress to represent the demands of the masses so that the voice of Congress could open up the deaf ears of the government and make them hear our suffering. Sir, allow me to tell you, one day all Europeans and the colonial government will have to leave this country. But we Asians will continue to live and trade in the country.

[Events in Uganda, many years later, did not quite work out as he had prophesied. AJ]

Hussein Suleman Verjee was arrested for his provocative words, but was spared imprisonment by Justice Sheridan who put him under house arrest for a while. I believe there is mention of this episode in HE Mohamed's book 'The Asian Legacy in Africa and The White Man's Colour Culture'."

The next chapter was played out when the Indian National Congress decided to send a delegation to London in 1923. The delegation consisted of Hussein Suleman Verjee along with famous names like MA Desai, AM Jivanjee, BS Verma, Mr Shamsudeen and Abdul Wahid. The Indian delegation from Kenya apparently stayed at the "First Avenue Hotel" in the Strand where they met a number of opposition British MPs who even entertained them to a lunch in their honour. Their representations for equal rights were disregarded by the British government and they came away empty handed.

POSTSCRIPT

A lot of water has flowed under the bridge since those days. It is the year 2007 as one reflects upon the past. And what is the racial equation today? In Kenya now, the Africans are the elite, for they govern their own country. Not all Africans belong to that category – not by a long chalk. There is the ruling and wealthy class. And there is a considerable African middle class. And there are vast numbers of Africans who might feel that their lot is no better than in the colonial days. And there are tribal divisions.

And there are too, still the Europeans and Indians, some of them extremely wealthy, though not quite so numerous. Schools, hospitals, Clubs and hotels are all open to people who can afford to pay for the services and facilities. There is greater friendliness and camaraderie between people of different races. There are genuine friendships between many individuals of different races. Interracial socialising is more evident in formal mixed-race parties and functions which are organised by Government bodies, Embassies, Service organisations like Rotary and Lions etc, Corporate bodies and the like. However, parties at home I have been to in Kenya tend to be single race gatherings with an occasional smattering of other races and communities. There are exceptions of course.

In terms of interracial and intercommunal marriages, Europeans appear to have become the most liberal, and the Indians remain the least. As I look around my own circle of acquaintances in East Africa, the UK and Canada (by no means to be taken as a representative sample), I come to the conclusion that European men and especially women are more willing to marry members of another race. I know of so many Africans and Afro-Carribeans with European wives, although there are fewer European males with African wives. From the same group, I can think of eight or nine Indian girls who have European husbands and an even bigger number of Indian men married to European girls. I personally know of only one Indian girl married to an African and one Indian having had an African wife. From this group I cannot think of too many Ismaili boys and girls who have spouses from other Indian communities. Nor for that matter do I know of too many marriages between Punjabis, Patels, Shahs, Bohoras, Memons or other Indian communities. I can remember the time, some fifty years ago, in Mombasa, when the son of a prominent Patel family got married to a girl from the Shah community, and that created quite a stir. They happened to be our very good friends, were happily married until the husband died recently.

MY LIFE IN ROTARY

IF I WERE TO MAKE A LIST OF HALF A DOZEN
OR SO THINGS WHICH MOST IMPACTED MY LIFE,
I HAVE NO DOUBT THAT MY FIFTY YEARS PLUS
INVOLVEMENT IN ROTARY WOULD BE HIGH UP ON THE LIST.
AND YET, AS I LOOK BACK ON MY ROTARY CAREER,
I REMEMBER HOW HARD I TRIED **NOT** TO JOIN ROTARY.
BUT LET ME START FROM THE BEGINNING...

ROTARY COMES TO KENYA

Rotary came to East Africa in 1930 when the Johannesburg Rotary Club sponsored the first Rotary Club in Nairobi. Until then, the African continent only had clubs in Johannesburg (1921/22), Salisbury, Cairo, Casablanca and Algeria. So the Nairobi Rotary Club was the first Rotary Club in what was then described as "Black Africa". (Paradoxically, in the 1930s, the only Africans around at Rotary meetings in Nairobi were the waiters at the New Stanley Hotel. And any Indians who set foot in the hotel would only have come through the Tradesmen's entrance.)

There were several reasons for the way in which the first Rotary Club in East Africa evolved. Firstly, the Johannesburg connection. A new Rotary club can only be formed when an existing club sponsors it - in this case, the South African club. Secondly, and, even more importantly, one can only become a Rotarian by invitation. One cannot apply for membership. Even an existing Rotarian, moving from one town to another, cannot automatically transfer his membership. Individuals become members of a specific Rotary Club; but only the clubs belong to what is known as Rotary International.

Then too there is the "Classification", principle which in those days had a narrow interpretation and was rigidly adhered to. Paul Harris, the founder of Rotary, a lawyer himself, wanted to create an "association" which would not be dominated by any one profession or trade, and so introduced the principle that every club could have only one member from any one trade or profession: one doctor, one lawyer, one coal merchant, one haberdasher, and so on. Additionally, the potential member had to be "an adult male of good character and reputation". The potential member also had to hold "a senior or an executive position" in a "leading and reputable" business or profession.

These rules provided the classic recipe for an elitist organisation, which reflected the social context of the colony of an imperial power - and perpetuated its stratified structure. This outcome might have been an unintended consequence – or not.

The Extension Officer from Johannesburg would only have met with European businessmen, professionals, farmers, Civil servants, administrators and so on in Nairobi. He would hardly have been taken for a drive through Indian Bazaar, or Ngara, nor would he have noticed the number of Indian shops beginning to appear on Government Road. The list of Charter members of the first Nairobi Rotary Club must have read like a Who's Who of the elite European establishment in Nairobi in 1930.

But it could not have been any different. There were no African professionals or businessmen in those days. There were Indian businessmen at the time, mostly traders and shopkeepers. It is inconceivable that any European Rotarian who valued his gin and tonic at the Muthaiga Club, would have had the temerity to propose an Indian for membership of the Nairobi Rotary Club in the nineteen-thirties.

And so the all-European Nairobi Rotary Club continued to fly the Rotary flag in Kenya, from 1930 until 1944, which included the war years. Clearly, Rotary extension was not uppermost on the minds of Nairobi Rotarians, for they were quite content to be the sole Rotary Club in Kenya for fourteen years, until 1944, when the Rotary Club of Mombasa came into being. Ironically, the first ever get-together of Rotarians in Mombasa took place at a lunch at the Mombasa Club, back in 1932, that is, two years after the Nairobi club was formed. Apparently, the President of Rotary International, Sydney W. Pascall, was passing through Mombasa. President Arthur Tannahill of Nairobi accompanied by other Nairobi Rotarians organised a lunch and invited leading Mombasa citizens to meet the RI President. There is no record of any non-Europeans having been invited. They could not have attended in any case, because the Mombasa Club was a Europeans-only establishment.

ROTARY IN MOMBASA

Officially, Nairobi Rotary Club is on record as having sponsored the Rotary Club in Mombasa. According to Edward Rodwell, however, the actual initiative to form a club in Mombasa was taken by one Charles Norman, who was the then District Commissioner of Mombasa. His previous posting had been in Palestine where he had been an active Rotarian and was in fact a Past President of the Jaffa-Tel Aviv Rotary Club whose membership consisted of Arabs, Jews and the British.

Charles Norman had seen at first hand how Rotary provided an opportunity for members of different communities to interact with each other, notwithstanding their differences – a kind of test-bed for the Fourth Object of Rotary. As the District Commissioner he was well placed to see the mix of communities, races and religions which made up the people of Kenya. There were the Europeans, mostly British expatriates, Hindus and Muslims of Indian origin, Arabs, and Somalis. And of course the Africans, who in turn belonged to various tribes, and the Coast Swahilis. He was determined to ensure that, unlike Nairobi, the Mombasa Rotary Club would reflect the population of the town as far as possible, within the rules of Rotary membership.

Given his determination and authority, and the fact that the political climate of Kenya was beginning to change, Charles Norman was successful, and the Mombasa Rotary Club received its Charter from Rotary International in 1944.

The following citizens of Mombasa were invited to become Charter Members of the new Mombasa Rotary Club. It is an historic list, for it shows the names and classifications of the members of the first genuinely multiracial Rotary Club in Africa, south of the Sahara.

Shariff Abdulla Salim - *Auctioning Services*
Samuel Reginald Boyd – *Civil Engineering*
Robert Sanford Campbell – *General Insurance*
Augustus Davies – *Coal Distribution*
Eric James Gibb – *Transportation Shipping*
Reginald Hawkins – *Land Administration*   SERGEANT-AT-ARMS
Mbarak Ali Hinawy – *Law-Arab Judicial*
Kassam Janmohamed – *Motion Picture Theatres* (THE REGAL)
Abdulhussein Kaderbhoy – *Cotton Ginning*
Shankar Dhondho Karve – *Medicine General*
James M Liston – *Public Health Services*
John Macintyre – *Municipal Engineering*   HON. SECRETARY
John Macleod – *Finance Banking*   HON. TREASURER
William George Nicol – *General Merchandise*
Charles B Norman – *Govt Administration*   PRESIDENT
Kassamali R Paroo – *Cotton Goods Distribution*
Ambalal B Patel – *Law General Practice*
Marinus A Pelt – *Consular Service*   VICE-PRESIDENT
Mohamed Ali Rana – *Muslim Association*
Eric Lewis Relf – *Accounting Services*
Percy H Selby – *Dairy Produce Distribution*
Amritlal U Sheth – *St John's Ambulance Association*
Arthur Thomas Walker – *Tobacco Distributing*

Conspicuous by their absence are any African names in the list of Charter Members. Despite his best efforts, Charles Norman could not find any Africans in Mombasa in 1944 who could satisfy the Classification Rules of Rotary. (James Mbotela became the first African Rotarian in Mombasa 24 years later, in 1968. He was a first class individual, and a personal friend of mine, and I hope to write more about him later on.) See pages 146 and 186.

Thus, my family and I became aware of Rotary for the first time when my father, Kassam Janmohamed, became a Charter Member of the Mombasa Rotary Club in 1944. I was thirteen then. Lunchtime in our household became a more relaxed affair on Tuesdays because my father would not join us, because he had "gone to Rotary" at the Manor Hotel, which was but a stone's throw from where we lived. His classification was Motion Picture Theatres. He was a keen and active Rotarian, with a perfect attendance, until his sudden and untimely death of a cerebral haemorrhage in 1950 at the age of forty-five.

This was a shattering experience for the family, especially my mother, who was then forty. The timing of my father's death was fateful. If my father had lived for just three more weeks, I would have been on board a ship, sailing to England for further studies, and it is probable that I would not even have learnt of his death until I reached England.

My mother demonstrated unexpected strength and determination, and dedicated her life to the welfare of her three children, Roshan (who was married by that time), Sultan and myself. I had no idea what aspirations my father had had for me. But my mother knew what she wanted of me. She wanted me to be as much like my father as possible, and she wanted me to take part in all the activities, business and social, which my father had been involved in. And foremost amongst this was Rotary. She knew the pleasure my father had derived from his membership of the Mombasa Rotary Club, and she wanted me to become a Rotarian - as soon as possible. I had no idea what Rotary was all about, or who other Rotarians were. The first time I saw a whole lot of them was at my father's funeral - apparently most of them had turned up. And I had a vague recollection of a whole clutch of soberly dressed, quite (to me) elderly gentlemen, Indians, Arabs and Europeans all wearing Rotary badges who came to the Ismaili cemetery on Makupa Road, to pay their last respects to a fellow Rotarian. They must have been important people, for a large number of them were mentioned by name in my father's Obituary notice in the Mombasa Times the following day.

ROTARY AND ME

Eventually my mother got around to telling me that she wanted me to join Rotary, "like your Bapa", she said. I was not enthusiastic. I had no desire to belong to a club where members were my father's age. She then spoke to Dr. Mohamedali Rana, a good family friend, Rotarian, and our partner in the City House. To my great relief, he explained to her that at the age of nineteen I was far too young to become a Rotarian. Most Rotarians were more than twice my age, and would never accept such a young boy into Rotary.

My mother revived the topic every so often, but to no avail. But she persisted, off and on, until 1956, when she finally prevailed upon Dr Rana to put my name forward as a Rotarian. There were one or two other prominent Rotarians who supported my name, and I believe I was somewhat grudgingly accepted into the Rotary Club of Mombasa in 1956. I had just turned twenty-five. My classification was Sports Goods Distribution.

(In fact, Six of the original Charter Members were still Rotarians in Mombasa when I was finally invited to join. They were Shariff Abdulla, Dr. Shanker Karve, Kassamali Paroo, Dr. Mohamedali Rana, Eric Relf and Dr. Amritlal Sheth, all contemporaries of my father.)

My worst fears were soon realised. There was a palpable generation gap. The youngest member of the club until I joined was a delightful chap called Dharampal Shanker Dass, who was at least fifteen years my senior. Others were much older. Literally, a generation separated me from them. Officers of the club and other Rotarians were unfailingly civil, but I did not belong in the camaraderie and fellowship of the club. Around the lunch table they discussed matters which I knew little about; they did business with each other; called each other by their first names; cracked unfunny jokes; and worked together in other organisations. Indeed, many of them were my father's contemporaries, and, in quite a few cases, had children who were older than me!

Amazingly, Rtn Kassamali Paroo remembered my very first day as a member of the Mombasa Rotary Club. He writes in his "diary":

"Now in Mombasa there was a young man called Ameer Kassam Janmohamed. In September 1956 he joined the Rotary Cub. I was the leader of the Ismaili community at the time, and at this time the debate of whether to smoke or not was very rife. Ameer came to the first luncheon meeting of the Rotary Club and happened to sit next to me. Across the table there was a European gentleman who offered a cigarette to Ameer. With great foresight Ameer declined the offer. I asked Ameer whether he smoked, and he said yes. I immediately remarked that since he was now a member of the Rotary Club, it followed that he did not need to demur in the club."

I told my mother repeatedly that I wanted to resign from Rotary. I was uncomfortable, and

Picture shows from left to right. Front row: Manohar Hosangady of Jubilee Insurance; Badruddin Alibhai Kanji – Building Contractors, District Governor Mello MacRobert, John Grootsveld of Tombooth, Devchand Chandaria – Industrialist, Becharbhai Patel – Hardwares; Frank Banham – Arab Boys School; and Ken Adcock – Mitchell Cotts. Back row: Unidentified Rtn; Dave Singer of Tudor House Hotel, myself (as the youngest member of the club), Doug Ratcliffe of Howse & McGeorge Chemists, Tom Burrows of Govt Coast Agency, and Unidentified Rtn.

I am sure the older members were too. And it was not as if I needed to belong. I played tennis at the United Sports Club and badminton at the Aga Khan club, and led a busy social life – with people in my own age group. My mother pleaded with me each time. "Give it some more time" she said, "You know how much it matters to me." And so I stayed on.

Opposite my shop, Badrudin's Sports House on Salim Road were the offices of M/s Karimjee Jivanjee Ltd, and Rtn Tayyabali Adamjee, who was my father's contemporary, asked me if I could give him a lift to the Tudor House Hotel and back every Tuesday for the Rotary lunch. This made me quite regular at Rotary lunches. He used to call me "dikra" meaning son. His son Hakim and I were friends – and later on in life more like brothers. But my feeling of isolation continued to grow and I continued to feel sorry for myself - until I had the great revelation! One day I suddenly realised something that should have been obvious to me right from the start. My not-so-young fellow Rotarians, though genuinely motivated by the Service concept of Rotary, in their white linen suits and ties, were not prone to rolling up their sleeves and volunteering when difficult jobs were on offer. I suddenly saw an opportunity to ingratiate myself by taking on jobs other Rotarians were unable or unwilling to undertake.

The first time I volunteered was when John Grootsveld, the President of the Rotary Club announced that the District Governor, Mello MacRobert from South Africa was due to visit the club. He had to be brought by car from Moshi to Mombasa. Ken Adcock had offered to provide a car. Would any Rotarian volunteer to go to Moshi to pick up the DG? It was a four hundred mile round trip, with a two nights' stay in Moshi. I volunteered. (Looking back on my Rotary career, I think that was a watershed moment). I drove Ken Adcock's Ford Zephyr to Moshi, attended the Moshi Rotary lunch the next day, and drove Mello MacRobert back to Mombasa on the following day. There were no tarmac roads in those days. Roads had corrugated surfaces with sandbanks in the middle and the sides, punctuated with potholes. It was also quite hair-raising when two vehicles crossed each other or overtook, because of clouds of dust which reduced visibility to nil. Despite all this, Mello enjoyed the drive to Mombasa. That was the first time that I had a one on one talk about Rotary with a senior Rotarian, and I think we both made lasting impressions on each other.

He was quite gracious and had good things to say about our exciting trip when he addressed the Mombasa Rotary club. He also spoke enthusiastically of the young Rotarian who had come to pick him up.

More Rotary jobs started coming my way - until there came a time when each year, incoming Committee chairmen vied with each other to have me on their committees! I had arrived! I was now regarded as "one of the boys".

FIRST INTER-ACT CLUB
ON THE AFRICAN CONTINENT

A major opportunity came my way in 1963 when AC Satchu was the President of the Club. That year, the President of Rotary International was Rtn Nitish Laharry from Bengal. Nitish was the first Indian to be elected President of RI. Amongst other things, he was promoting the idea of Inter-Act Clubs as an opportunity for boys and girls in the last three years of their secondary education to be introduced to the idea of practical Community Service and International Service under the aegis of local Rotary Clubs.

President AC Satchu received the "bumpf" on the Inter-Act programme from RI, and probably as I was the youngest member (I was 32 then), asked me if I would like to have a crack at it. This was tailor made for me. Apart from being a Rotarian, I was an ex-student of the Aga Khan High School in Mombasa, and was now also a member of the Aga Khan Education Board. I approached Gus Corkery, Headmaster of the school. He thought it was an excellent idea. To cut a long story short, the Aga Khan High School and the Mombasa Rotary Club had the privilege of forming what became the first Interact Club on the African Continent. The first President of the Inter-Act Club was young Zulfiqar S Mangalji, who was succeeded by Salim Somani in the following year.

That year, 1964, Salim and I made a presentation at a Rotary District Conference in Kitwe in Zambia. The concept and the presentation were enthusiastically received. The idea took off - and this was the beginning of the spread of Inter-Act Clubs throughout the continent. At the time of writing this, I understand there are now more than ten thousand inter-act clubs in 109 countries of the world with a memebership of 220,000. I was elected President of the Mombasa Rotary Club for 65/66. I was thirty-four at the time.

With AC Satchu and Anant Pandya at District Assembly in Moshi in 1960. Foothills of Mt. Kilimanjaro in the background.

Rotarians and wives at Port Reitz Airport waiting to greet visitors for conference. Zeenat, myself, Hansa Pandya, Anant Pandya behind her, Sir Charles Mortimer, Bill Keymer behind him, John Longman behind lady, and Ted Stairs, Editor Of Mombasa Times at far right back. Sir Charles Mortimer was District Governor in 1955/56 when the District also included Southern Rhodesia and South Africa.

It was an exciting year because we had the challenge of hosting the first ever Rotary District Conference in Mombasa. We had this privilege because the District Governor for the year was the charismatic Anant Pandya, a member of our club, who had the distinction of being the first non-European to become a Rotary Governor in Africa south of the Sahara. At the time I was also concurrently the Mukhi of the Mombasa Jamat Khana. Any person who accepts the post of Mukhi or Kamadia in an Ismaili Jamat Khana automatically undertakes to attend Jamat Khana at prayer times every evening, unless he is out of town, or unwell. This presented me with a problem, because as the President of the Host Club, my presence was also required at evening functions during the District Conference. I took my quandary to Count Fatehali Dhala, who was the most senior member of our Communal hierarchy. Count Fatehali, ever the pragmatist, solved my dilemma by assuring and comforting me that my absence from Jamat Khana for those four days, when I was discharging my responsibility as the President of the Host Rotary Club, would not be seen as a dereliction of duty by the Community. Quite the contrary - and I should harbour no feelings of guilt.

The District Conference, held in the Indian Women's Association Hall, was a great success. Hon Charles Njonjo represented the President of Kenya.

THE "UNCLE" SYNDROME

Notwithstanding my acceptance and progress in the Mombasa Rotary Club, I still struggled with one particular aspect of Rotary. With a view to promoting fellowship and camaraderie, Rotarians throughout the world address each other by their first names. However I could not bring myself to address Count Paroo as Kassamali, Dr. Rana as Mohamedali, AC Satchu as AC, or Dr. Karve as Shanker. These guys were my father's contemporaries after all, and in keeping with the time honoured Indian custom I used to call them "uncle". The problem became more acute when I became the President. It is customary for the President to say, "I now call upon Eric, or John, or whomever, to say Grace, or welcome the visitors, or thank the speaker, or to propose the Loyal Toast. Since I could not address these "uncles" of mine by their first names, I simply stopped allocating duties to them! Count Paroo was the first one to notice this. In his typically forthright manner he asked me why I never asked him to perform any of those duties. I explained my dilemma to him. His response was that in the Community context he would find it extraordinary if I addressed him, or referred to him as Kassamali. However, he said I could call him Kassamali from the Chair at Rotary. I rather used to relish saying from the Chair, "I now call upon Kassamali to welcome the visitors" …

I ran this past some other "uncles", but not all of them were comfortable about being addressed by their first names by me. Dear Dr. Rana (who was my original sponsor) told me not to be a "gaddha" about it. Dr. Karve Sr, however, was quite happy to be addressed as Shanker.

School for Blind Children

Amongst a number of initiatives, I fondly remember one Rotary project during my year as President. This was the building of the Salvation Army School for blind children in Likoni, not far from the old ferry ramp on the mainland side. I was approached at the beginning of my year by Rtn Len Millar, who was a Canadian and was in charge of the Salvation Army activities in the Coast Province. He told me that the Kenya Government, in response to their requests, had recently allocated a plot of land in Likoni to them to build a school for blind children. The Salvation Army had the wherewithal to run such a school, and now had the land. What was missing was a school building, to consist of some dormitories and class rooms. Would I consider making this the main Community Service project of my year? My Board of Directors were enthusiastic and we adopted the idea as our Community Service project for the year. At first we decided to take the conventional approach and raise funds for the buildings. But then events took an interesting turn.

I happened to mention the project to Rtn Roberts who was the Managing Director of the British Standard Portland Cement Company, and half in jest, asked him if his company would consider donating some cement? He said, "You come and visit the cement plant in Bamburi one day, and on your return journey, you can take away all the cement you can carry." I discussed this with my friend Rtn Yusuf Mamujee of Mamujee Brothers, timber and building materials merchants. He suggested he would accompany me to the cement plant in Bamburi, and that we should go there in one of his company's pick-ups! Rtn Roberts was not at all put out when I turned up at his plant in a pick-up, although he did admit later that he was rather expecting me to turn up in my Peugeot 404 saloon! He rose to the occasion magnificiently, however, and actually instructed his men to load the pick-up with bags of BSPCC cement. He also invited us to feel free to ask for more.

Inspired by this spontaneous generosity, Yusuf Mamujee said he was sure that his firm too, could supply timber and other building materials free of charge for the project. The next question was - who would actually construct the dormitories and class rooms which were required? We both came up with the same answer. Past President Rtn Badrudin Alibhai Kanji, of Alibhai Kanji and Co, Building Contractors! (Their firm had already built the New City House for us in 1957) We put the proposal to Badrubhai. When he learnt that we already had most of the building materials, he suggested we meet with Len Millar at the Salvation Army to ascertain the design of the school and the extent of construction. Further, Rtn Badrudin Kanji said, "We shall build the school ourselves."

We had the required school buildings ready in ten months. Mombasa Rotarians were also able to provide some nice touches for the school. Rtn Jimmy Vaghela of M/s Stylo offered to provide uniforms for the first batch of blind boys and girls. Rtn Dharampal Shankerdass offered to provide musical instruments for a school orchestra. And not to be outdone, our ladies got into the act in a big way. Our wives used to operate as the Inner Wheel Club (Rotary was an all male organisation at the time). They set up a programme to visit the school on a regular basis and establish personal contacts with individual boys and girls, to create voice recognition relationships with them. Zeenat (who was the President of the Inner Wheel at the time) was ably assisted in the project by a number of Inner Wheelers, who included Pamela Grubb, wife of the British High

From left to right: Pamela Grubb, Mrs Millar, behind her Nillie Austin and Major Osborne. Boys and girls who were the first intake of blind children to join the school. Mrs Osborne, Zeenat and Sheila Hira on the extreme right.

Commissioner representative in Mombasa, Sheila, wife of Rtn Kishu Hira (whose father was also a Rotarian) of Sindh General Stores, and Nillie, wife of Rtn Elchie Austin of Austin Electrical Services, and Mrs Len Miller, among others.

The Salvation Army School for Blind Children at Likoni was formally handed over to the Army at a special ceremony by District Governor Anant Pandya on behalf of the Mombasa Rotary Club in 1966. Emblazoned on a side wall of the administration building was a large concrete Rotary wheel. Len Millar said blind children would be able to feel the wheel with their hands when he explained Rotary to them!

FATHERS AND SONS

I have mentioned that Kishu and his father Narain Hira were both Rotarians in Mombasa at the same time. In fact, over a period of time there have been several father and son combinations who were members of the Mombasa Rotary club simultaneously. They were Hon Ambalal Patel and Chiman Lal Patel, both lawyers; AC Satchu and Mansur Satchu, both lawyers; Dr. Shanker Karve and Madhav Karve, both doctors; Narain Hira and Kishu Hira, both in the same business: Kassamali Paroo and Amir Paroo - though with different classifications. (This was only possible because the Classification rules of Rotary had in the meantime been relaxed with the creation of Additional Active members and Major and Minor Classifications). Although my father and I were both members of the Mombasa Rotary Club, I did not join Rotary until six years after my father's death.

District Governorship

I shall never forget that evening in 1967, when the phone rang in our flat in City House, Mombasa. It was the then District Governor Jo Lloyd, speaking from his home in Tanga. He said he had just returned from his visits to the clubs in the District and that the College of Governors would like to put my name forward as the Governor of our District for the year 1969/70. Would I accept the nomination, subject of course to ratification by the next District Conference? For me, at the age of 36, this was an extraordinary opportunity, for what was being offered was the potential Governorship of what was geographically the largest Rotary District in the world, consisting of nine African and Indian Ocean countries. Zeenat and I did not take too long to say yes to Jo Lloyd. I was returned unopposed at the next District Conference which confirmed me as the DG Nominee for 1969/70.

A number of things have to happen before a DG Nominee becomes a fully fledged District Governor. First, he has to give an undertaking to the Secretariat of Rotary International at Evanston, Illinois, USA, that he will attend the International Assembly for the full duration, before he takes office, and will, without fail, visit every single Rotary club in his District, at least once during his term of office, and more in case of need. It is, essentially, an undertaking to commit full time almost two years of your life to Rotary.

In my case, it meant my having to attend the International Assembly in the U.S., followed by the International Convention in Honolulu, and then to make visits to Rotary Clubs in my District. Going to Uganda and Tanzania was not a problem, but travel to Zambia, Malawi and the Indian Ocean countries was considered foreign travel. So a would-be District Governor in Kenya had to contend with this additional problem in 1969 - the

123

problem of currency. Travelling out of Kenya meant having to pay in foreign exchange, and the Central Bank of Kenya only sanctioned foreign exchange when the journey in question was demonstrably for the economic benefit of Kenya. Travels undertaken by Rotary District Governors were not viewed in this light.

According to the rules of RI, District Governors were entitled to one first class fare for all their travels if they travelled on their own, or as Rotary preferred, two economy class fares if they were accompanied by their wives. (The concept of Club Class had not yet emerged). Rotary International came to my rescue when they were informed of my predicament. They remitted my anticipated expenses each time in foreign currency, against which the Central Bank would allow my travel agents to issue tickets for overseas travel.

On one occasion at least, there was some embarrassment and considerable mirth due to Zeenat and myself travelling economy class. This was during our very first visit to Mauritius. Our plane from Nairobi landed at Port Louis airport. Zeenat and I disembarked from the rear door of the plane along with all other economy class passengers. We did notice that there was considerable excitement on the tarmac near the steps leading to the First Class exit of the plane. There was a red carpet, TV cameras, and a group of smartly dressed people. Clearly they were expecting some VIPs. We walked into the airport terminal and much to our dismay found no signs of any Rotarians to receive us. I was concerned, because the Port Louis Rotary Club had undertaken to organise my District Conference and this was not an auspicious sign. Upon enquiring, we learnt that the Rotarians and their ladies, along with a number of civic dignitaries were on the tarmac, to receive their District Governor!

The International Assembly is a euphemism for what is really a "school" for incoming District Governors from all over the world. In my year (1969), the Assembly was held at the Lake Placid Country Club in upper New York State. There were 106 incoming DGs from fifty-two countries from all five Continents. It is a place where committed Rotarians, nominated by their respective Districts, are "Informed, Instructed and Inspired". They are taught, amongst other things, how to improve their skills in communication and public speaking. They then go on to the International Convention where the Convention will elect them. From the status of DG Nominee, they then become DG Elect. Thereafter they return to their respective Districts where they are installed as fully fledged District Governors, and receive their Chain of Office, in the presence of Rotarians of their District assembled at an Annual Conference.

During the International Assembly, which lasts one week, incoming DGs get to know the hierarchy of Rotary International and to meet their fellow incoming District Governors from all over the world. Zeenat and I met many fine people and made many lasting friendships, too numerous to mention. I will make one exception, however, in the case of one of the finest human beings I have ever had the privilege to meet (see next section).

To facilitate participants getting to know each other as quickly as possible, RI produces a Directory of all participants in the International Assembly each year, with their photos and brief biographies. Zeenat and I studied our copy of the Directory as soon as we arrived at Lake Placid. The Directory makes formidable reading because participants are mostly individuals who have made their marks, not only in Rotary, but in the communties and countries where they came from.

KASSIM DADA

We came across one name, Kassim Dada, who was the DG Nominee from Pakistan. (At that time Pakistan consisted of West and East Pakistan). We were tickled because our son's name is also Quassim, and we made it a point to seek out Kassim Dada on the very first evening. This was in May 1969. I am proud to say that we formed a bond of friendship from that very first meeting which endured until his untimely death in March 2001.

He was possessed of that rarest of qualities in highly gifted individuals, humility. The International Assembly Directory described him with the following words:

"KASSIM DADA, Shirin Manzil, Randal Road, Karachi, 3, Pakistan – Governor Nominee, District 307, RI. A native of Bombay, India, Kassim graduated from St Xavier's College in Calcutta. Since 1949, Kassim has held a variety of executive industrial positions, leading to his current position as Chairman of Asbestos Cement Industries Ltd. He is President of the All Pakistan Memon Federation and past Director of the Pakistan Refugee Rehabilitation Finance Corporation. Kassim is President of the Karachi Stock Exchange, and a member of the cement products advisory panel for the Ministry of Industries. He is past chairman of the Pakistan Ship-Owners Association. A Rotarian since 1954, Kassim is a member and past president of the Rotary Club of Karachi."

I subsequently learnt, but not from him, that his company owned cement plants in East and West Pakistan and he used to fly his own plane when he visited the plants. He also sat as a Director on the Pakistani Boards of several international companies such as Cessna Aircraft, Jensen-Nicholson, and Brooke Bond Tea. Notwithstanding his achievements and the obvious respect he enjoyed from all those who knew him, I never heard Kassim talk about himself. He was sincerely interested in other people. You knew that he was genuinely listening when others talked. He was the perfect embodiment of dignity and self-respect, without an iota of ego.

Kassim and I travelled together from Lake Placid to Honolulu for the International Convention, where both of us were formally elected. We then met up in Karachi where he had arranged for me to address the Karachi Rotary Club before my return to Nairobi for my own installation as the Governor of District 220.

In the ensuing years, Kassim and I continued to meet regularly, occasionally when I visited Karachi, but mostly when he passed through London on his way to Rotary International Councils and the like. My lasting picture of Kassim is of him sitting on that little stool in the corner of Whiteman's Dairy in Holland Street in Kensington, when he came to visit me; and of the number of times when he actually served customers when we got busy near closing time!

And I say this without embarrassment - that knowing him has hugely enriched my life. Perhaps the finest compliment to Kassim was paid by Rtn Rajendra Saboo of Chandigar,

With Kassim (next to me) and family in Karachi. Hanifa Bahen in the middle in front row.

127

India, who was the President of Rotary International 1991/1992. I was privileged to meet Rajendra at his hotel in London quite fortuitously. His London representative happened to be a tenant of mine in Putney! When he learnt that I was a past District Governor from Africa and a Past President of the Kensington Rotary Club, he arranged for me to meet his "boss", who was particularly interested in contributions made to Rotary in different parts of the world by people of Indian origin. We were talking Rotary over coffee, when I happened to mention Kassim Dada. Rajendra said he had been privileged to work with Kassim on various Rotary International committees and he knew of no better man in the sub-Continent to be the President of Rotary International than Kassim Dada.

DISTRICT 220

Being elected as the Governor of a Rotary International District is a unique experience. The world of Rotary is divided into Districts for administrative purposes. Each District has a Governor, elected by Rotarians in the District, who represents the President and the Board of Rotary International in his District and he is known as an Officer of Rotary International in the region in which he operates.

Districts come in different shapes and sizes. For instance, one of the smallest geographical Districts, but with the largest number of clubs was District 113, which covered Greater London, with nearly ninety clubs.

In my case, my District 220 was the largest geographical Rotary District covering nine African and Indian Ocean countries, but had only 31 clubs at the beginning of my year. I was privileged to present Charters to three new Rotary Club during my year. They were Kampala West in Uganda, Tananarive-Anosy in Madagascar and Lilongwe in Malawi. So I ended my term with 34 clubs in the District. Purely for historical record, District 220 in 1969/1970 consisted of the following clubs:

KENYA: Kisumu, Mombasa, Nairobi, Nairobi South, Nairobi North, Nakuru
UGANDA: Jinja, Kampala, Kampala West, Mbale
TANZANIA: Arusha, Daressalaam, Moshi, Tanga
MALAWI: Blantyre, Lilongwe
ZAMBIA: Chingola, Kabwe, Kitwe, Livingstone, Luanshya, Lusaka, Ndola, Mufulira
MADAGASCAR: Diego Suarez, Majunga, Tananarive, Tananarive-Anosy, Tamatave, Tulear

Presentation of the Charter to the President of the Lilongwe Rotary Club – 1969.

MAURITIUS: Port Louis
LA RE-UNION: Saint Denis, Saint-Benoit
COMORES: Moroni

With the exception of La Re-Union, which was still a "Department" of Metropolitan France, all other eight countries had achieved independence from their colonial masters within the previous few years. Rotary was viewed with mixed sentiments in different countries, but was largely viewed as a Europeans-only, colonial inheritance. Clubs in some countries had progressed to multi-racial memberships, notably Kenya (with one exception), Uganda and Tanzania.

Zambia had a handful of Asian Rotarians in some Copper Belt Clubs. As President Kaunda himself pointed out to us at the opening of a District Conference in 1967 at Ndola, he had been roundly criticised by parts of the Zambian press for agreeing to formally open a Rotary District Conference, given that there wasn't a single black Zambian Rotarian in the country. He went on to say that he supported the objects of Rotary, and he hoped that Rotary would one day flourish in Zambia, with the involvement of more and more Zambians.

Madagascar had begun to accept non-European members into Rotary. Clubs in Malawi, La Re-Union and the Comores had an all white membership.

This commemorative plate was given to me by Rotarians of Madagascar in 1969 as a memento of my visit. The 1770 map shows the Mozambique Channel, the island of Madagascar and Eastern coast of Africa, which were part of District 220 of which I was the Governor. The Comores are situated between Madagascar and the African mainland. To the East is the island of Mauritius, which was then known as Isle de France.

With President Kenneth Kaunda at Rotary Conference in Ndola, Zambia in April 1967.

Rotary in Moroni, Comores

The one Rotary Club in Moroni, the capital of the Grande Comores is worth mentioning. The Comorian Islands had been under French rule until independence. The vast majority of the population consisted of Arab Muslims, a fair number of Indians, and a small number of French Europeans. Moroni reminded me of Zanzibar, with numerous Mosques and the sounds of the Muezzins calling the faithful to prayers from lofty minarets.

The Comores were known as large exporters of an exotic tropical flower called Ylangilang, also known as Langi-Langi. The essence of this flower is used as the base for perfumes. The biggest market for these flowers was in France, especially the perfume makers of Grasse. And as one Comorian explained to me, the economy of the country consequently depended largely on the price the perfumieres of Grasse were prepared to pay for the flower in any given year. This also explained the status of the handful of French who lived in the Islands. Although France had conceded sovereignty, the Islands were very much in the French sphere of influence, both economically and culturally. The average man on the street had a smattering of French, besides his native tongue, for example, Arabic, Gujarati, Hindi, and even Kiswahili! The country had historical links with Oman, Muscat and India, as did Zanzibar.

The Moroni Rotary Club consisted exclusively of white French men. They were mostly from Metropolitan France and represented various French interests on the Islands. They were good fun, although they had a somewhat cavalier attitude toward the rules of Rotary. As the District Governor I felt it incumbent upon me to comment on some of their unusual interpretations of the rules. They disarmingly informed me that they considered that there was too much "Anglo-Saxon regimentation" in the way Rotary operated!

Their principle project had been to construct a beautiful Club House for themselves! It was wonderfully situated atop a rocky promontory overlooking the Indian Ocean. I told them that I found this contrary to the spirit of Rotary - Service above Self and all that. However, they had a plausible reason. They said that there was no decent place on the island where a Rotary club could meet each week and where Rotarians could expect a decent meal with a good wine list. So they had raised money from within themselves and built the Club house. We agreed that the Club house could perhaps be regarded as a Community Service project if other organisations could also be allowed to use the premises for their activities.

The Moroni Rotary Club had arranged for me to pay my respects to the President of the Comores, Said Mohammed Sheikh. Since I spoke no Arabic and only very basic French, the Rotary Club President had to double as the interpreter. In response to his question as to what I thought of his country, I told him that I saw much beauty and lovely flowers everywhere. His response was both sad and poetic. He sighed and said, "If only we could eat flowers and drink beauty." He wanted to know about the activities of Rotary in general and the Moroni Club in particular. I was able to tell him that the local club had decided to share their Clubhouse with other organisations and had also decided to embark on two local community service projects. One was to create facilities to catch and collect rain water, and secondly to build a modern paediatric ward to be attached to the local hospital.

The President was obviously intrigued by me. I was the first Muslim non-European, District Governor he had met. He was curious about my name and my background. He even told me about the recent visit of His Highness the Aga Khan to the islands. To my great – and pleasant – surprise, he asked the Club President to stay on for a while longer because he wanted to make a presentation to me. He gave instructions to an aide, who re-appeared with a small package on a silver salver. He then asked everyone to be upstanding - and pinned a Decoration on my jacket, at the same time giving me a beautifully inscribed certificate which states that I am now "un Officier de l'Ordre du Croissant Vert des Comores". Which is to say, he created me an Officer of the Order of the Green Crescent of the Comores!

I expect every Rotary District Governor, especially of a District as diverse and spread-out as mine was, could tell many interesting stories about his experiences. I have to curb my enthusiasm, for I could easily end up by writing a whole book about my Rotary experiences. So, I shall content myself by briefly touching upon one or two other items which left an imprint on my mind.

A CHILL WIND IN NAKURU

I was formally installed as the Governor of Rotary International District 220 at the Annual District Conference held in All Saints Cathedral in Nairobi in June 1969. The outgoing Governor was Graham Clarke, of Nairobi South. He asked me if the two of us could meet on our own after the Conference, for he felt he should tell me something which I ought to bear in mind as I travelled through our District.

We met for coffee the following morning. He was clearly ill at ease, for he had very kindly, and bravely, taken it upon himself to talk to me about an ugly subject in words which I might find least offensive. As he put it, whilst Rotary Clubs in our part of the world were gradually moving towards becoming multi-racial, not all clubs were reacting in the same manner. Most clubs had embraced this. Others were accepting the inevitable with as much grace as they could muster. There were one or two clubs however, which were not reconciled to the idea; and they were going to find it difficult to countenance an official visit from a non-European District Governor. He felt I ought to bear this in mind as I did my rounds of the District.

With some reluctance, he agreed to give me the names of the two clubs where he thought I might anticipate problems. One was Lusaka in Zambia, and the other was Nakuru in Kenya! To this day, I am grateful to PDG Graham Clarke for having warned me. It gave me time to think about the matter and be as prepared as one can be in a situation such as this.

In those days, the District Governor's official visit to each club was in three parts. First he met with the President and the Hon Secretary to assess the strengths and weaknesses of the club. Then there was a Club Assembly where the DG would meet the membership, discuss problems if any, make suggestions, and engage in a question and answer session about Rotary generally. Lastly, there would be a formal dinner or lunch, with ladies present, and it generally included local dignitaries and the press. This was the opportunity for the DG to talk about Rotary the world over, and generally deliver an "inspirational" address, laced with humour, and tailored to the community and the country in which the Club functioned.

In the event, my visit to the Lusaka Club went smoothly, helped perhaps by the fact that I was personally known to a number of their members whom I had met at District Conferences in Kitwe and Ndola in previous years.

Nakuru was another story. The all-white membership of the club consisted of land-owners, farmers, businessmen, and professionals, many of whom appeared to have South African backgrounds or connections. Seven years after Kenya's independence, they had not succeeded in identifying a single non-European for membership of the Nakuru Rotary club. They all lived on their farms or ranches outside Nakuru. Only Indians and Africans lived in the township.

Pictures show
Zeenat in her Rotary sari
at other
Rotary functions

The formal dinner of the Nakuru Rotary Club proved to be quite interesting. Zeenat and I arrived at the Stag's Head Hotel at the appointed time and were met by the bachelor President of the Rotary Club. We saw a large, all-European gathering and the President said that almost all the members and their wives, plus a large number of guests, were present. He escorted us to the bar and organised drinks for us. We exchanged a few pleasantries, and then he had to excuse himself, for a Club President has many things to attend to on an evening such as this. Zeenat and I looked around. I was pleasantly surprised at the large gathering. The Rotarians and their ladies stood in a loose semi-circle around us, but at a distance, and we were left pretty much to our own devices.

The only other person who came up to talk to us was an Indian – yes, Indian – Rotarian! His name was Vinoo Thakore if I'm not mistaken. He was a visiting Rotarian from Arusha and was in Nakuru on an extended business visit. He said he was proud of his regular attendance and had continued to make up his attendance at the Nakuru club every week. He had a sense of humour, for he suggested that I should recommend him for a decoration - for masochism - from Rotary International, for making up attendance at a club which made it quite obvious that he was not welcome.

I could see that there was curiosity about Zeenat and I - surreptitious glances in our direction and the general body language. Zeenat as usual, looked resplendent, especially in her Rotary Sari. She had had it specially embroidered in Bombay, when we were returning from the RI Convention in Honolulu. It was a white silk sari with a design of discreet Rotary emblems, tastefully embroidered in gold and blue beads. It had wowed Rotarians and their ladies in the thirty-three other Rotary Clubs we had already visited before coming to Nakuru. The Nakuru Rotarians must have wondered a little about me too, for apart from being of a different colour, I was clearly the youngest Rotarian in the room.

After an uncomfortable, and what seemed to be an interminable wait, the President eventually returned and escorted us to the top table, for the dinner was to commence. I noticed that fellowship within the club was good, so long as you were white. Zeenat had warned me to be extra careful when having soup, for I had this propensity to decorate my shirt-front or tie with the soup of the day. Previously there had been this one horrible occasion when I had spoken to a club oblivious of the fact that the end of my tie bore the unmistakable marks of having been dipped in the cream of tomato earlier on!

Finally, it was time for me to address the gathering. The Loyal Toast, to President Kenyatta, had been proposed, and the club President made the customary introduction. The table arrangement consisted of the top table with four extensions, rather like an "E" with four legs, so that half the audience had their backs to me when I stood up to speak. I noticed from the outset that none of the people with their backs to me made any attempt to adjust their chairs, so that they could face me, not even sideways, when I stood up to speak. And those who were facing me, studiously avoided looking at me as I spoke! Also - most of them busied themselves lighting cigars and cigarettes!

Thanks however to the forewarning from Graham Clarke, I was mentally well prepared for calculated indifference verging on hostility. I had intentionally left Nakuru to the last, so that I could be better prepared. I had already addressed thirty-three other clubs in nine countries, and I had my speech well prepared and polished. And also, I had so much of interest to tell them about Rotary, not only in our own, rather fascinating District, but throughout the world. I don't believe that the Nakuru Rotarians could have faulted me on the content of my speech, nor on my command of English. About five minutes into my speech, the first few chairs began to turn slightly so that the incumbents could look at me better. There was that distinctive scraping sound on wooden floors. I became aware that more people were now beginning to look in my direction, and listening. I knew I had their attention when I even elicited half-laughs at some of my jokes. The Rotarian who was charged with returning thanks to the speaker even managed to sound sincere when he thanked me for an "interesting and inspiring" speech.

At the end of the meeting, as Zeenat and I were preparing to take our leave - we did not have too many people to say good-bye to - the President of the club asked if we would stay on for a while because he was sure that a number of Rotarians and their wives would "love" to have a drink with us. Perhaps an olive branch was being offered. But Zeenat and I were too exhausted to accept the invitation and took our leave - with both my tie and my shirt-front without a mark on them. Perhaps we missed out on an opportunity to improve race relations in Nakuru. However!

THE FLYING DOCTOR
SERVICES OF TANZANIA

Amongst so many, one of the more rewarding experiences during my term of office was the handing over of a Cessna Ambulance Aeroplane to the Flying Doctor Services of Tanzania, run by the African Medical and Research Foundation.

Apparently, sometime in the early sixties, an American Rotarian, on a safari in Tanzania, wanted to buy films for his camera and walked into an Indian chemist's shop in Moshi. Whilst waiting to be served he noticed a framed Rotary Four-Way Test displayed along with the chemist's certificates on the wall.

For the benefit of the uninitiated, the Rotary Four-Way test reads as follows:

Is it the TRUTH?
Is it FAIR to all concerned?
Will it build GOODWILL and BETTER FRIENDSHIPS?
Will it be BENEFICIAL to all concerned?

(The Rotary Four-Way Test was created in 1932 by Rtn Herbert Taylor, and formally adopted by Rotary International in 1943 as a guide for high ethical standards in businesses and professions, and applied to the things we think, say and do).

He discovered that the owner of the shop was Rotarian Moti Malde and went along with him to the next meeting of the Moshi Rotary Club. There he learnt that the Moshi Rotary Club was trying to raise funds to buy a spare propeller for one of the air-planes belonging to the Flying Doctor Services. The American Rotarian happened to belong to a club in southern California which had a strong Flying Fellowship. He was absolutely tickled by what he had learnt. Upon his return to his home club he talked about the Moshi Rotary Club Community Service project. They wanted to get involved. Why just a propeller? Why not an entire ambulance aeroplane?

This was the spark that ignited what went on to become a World Community Service project, as more and more Clubs wanted to be part of this wonderful project, spearheaded by the Rotary clubs of Moshi and Arusha. By a happy co-incidence, the Presidents of both clubs were good friends of mine. Moshi President was Dr. Ram Paonaskor, and Akbar Natha Hirji was the President of the Arusha Rotary Club that year. Akbar's wife Khatun (nee Paroo) was an ex-Mombasa girl and we used to play badminton for many years for the Aga Khan Club in Mombasa.

I had been briefed about this project before I went to Lake Placid for the International Assembly. There I met up with the incoming Governors of the Districts which were supporting this project, especially Southern California, New Jersey and London. We were able to put the final touches to the project and finalise the logistics.

The project came to fruition in February 1970 at a ceremony at Moshi Airport when the Cessna 206 Ambulance plane was handed over to the Junior Minister of Health in Tanzania, Miss Lucy Lameck, who received the keys on behalf of the Flying Doctor Service and the Tanzania Government. The plane was aptly named "The Spirit of Rotary".

East African Standard

Monday, February 23, 1970.   Nairobi, Tel. 57633 (City Office 26421)
Reporters 26421

Picture shows Miss Lucy Lameck, Junior Minister for Health in the Tanzania Government, being received by the District Governor at Moshi Airport, to accept the Rotary Flying Ambulance on behalf of the African Medical and Research Foundation.

This is what I had to say on that occasion:

"International understanding….Ideal of service as a basis of worthy enterprise…high ethical standards…world fellowship of business and professional men…With its exotic terminology, the object of Rotary has at times been accused of pomposity by the uninitiated. And then, along comes a moment such as this, when a world fellowship of business and professional men, united in the ideal of service, promotes international understanding with a tangible exemplification of service which knows no frontiers.

We bear witness to a proud moment, not only for the few Moshi and Arusha Rotarians, but all Rotarians from many and distant lands whose dedication and sacrifice have made this day possible.

The dedication of a flying ambulance on this day is particularly appropriate. An aircraft on wings, on an errand of mercy, is symbolic of all that Rotary stands for. It symbolises the soaring human spirit, struggling to free itself from the shackles of disease, ignorance, poverty and misunderstanding. It is a vivid example of how Rotary's internationality helps combat these evils. Perhaps it is also a vindication of lofty ideals.

Another glorious chapter has been added to the annals of Rotary history. It will serve to spur us on to even greater efforts in a spirit of deep humility."

A Memorable
Occasion for Rotary

H. H. Aga Khan address to Rotary Clubs
of Karachi and Hyderabad-Feb 1976.

His Highness concluded his address to the Rotarians and other guests by making the following announcement.

"…Finally, Ladies and Gentlemen, I am happy to announce this evening what I hope, in the fullness of time, will become a major influence on the evolution of the Muslim cultural heritage.

It concerns the art form in which I have taken a deep personal interest for many years. Beginning in 1980, and every three years thereafter, I propose to offer a substantial monetary prize to the architect who has completed a building which most successfully embraces the spirit of Muslim architecture…It will be open to architects of any nationality who have designed and completed Muslim buildings in any country of the world, and will thus be truly international in scope.

The criteria on which the prize is awarded, the method of adjudication and the organizations who should be concerned are matters for discussion by the appropriate bodies…"

I will conclude, Ladies and Gentlemen, by saying how much I have enjoyed this occasion tonight and by wishing the members of the Clubs represented here this evening, continued success in the many activities you undertake, as well as the good causes to which you offer such generous help and assistance".

H.H. Aga Khan as guest of honour at inter-city meeting of Rotary clubs of Karachi and Hyderabad in Pakistan Feb. 1976.

P.D.G. Kassim Dada presenting Mrs. Zeenat, wife of P.D.G. Ameer Janmohamed to His Highness at the meeting. Rotary Four-Way Test in the background.

THE FOUR-WAY TEST IN BANGKOK

Many years later, in 1980, Zeenat and I had stopped over in Bangkok on our way back from Melbourne. We met up with our very dear friends Sadru and Zarin Gulamani who were returning from a trip to the Far East. We had planned that we would meet up at the Thai Intercontinental Hotel in Bangkok. The hotel foyer had the inevitable array of boutiques, with seductive displays of tempting goodies to attract foreign visitors. Zeenat and Zarin were instinctively attracted to the shop selling pearls. The salesperson persuaded them that if they wanted to see a much larger selection of pearls, they should really visit their main branch which was situated in the heart of Bangkok.

Naturally Sadru and I were not terribly enthusiastic, but the salesperson overcame our reluctance by offering us a ride in their company limousine for the trip to their main showroom downtown and back. The shop was called "Nelson Alexander", named after its founder. Whilst Zeenat and Zarin were engrossed in the selection of pearls, I walked around the emporium, and there on the wall behind the cashier's desk, prominently displayed, I saw a framed Rotary Four-Way Test! Upon enquiring I was told that the owner, Mr. Nelson Alexander, was a keen Rotarian. Could I get to see him, I asked. I was told that he was actually at a Rotary lunch at the time but should be back in a few minutes.

Nelson came back shortly and we chatted, and I mentioned that I was a Past District Governor of Rotary. Then he said that he was actually the Governor-nominee for his District, which consisted of a number of clubs in Thailand and Malaysia, and in fact he was to go to Lake Placid in a couple of months to attend the International Assembly! He was interested and I was able to fill him in about life at Lake Placid during an International Assembly.

I gave him the names of two other Rotarians who were also going to be at the Assembly that year. First was PDG Kassim Dada, from Pakistan who was going there as a Tutor. And the second was Pip Barnes from Mombasa, who was going there as the Governor-nominee of my old District. I was delighted that the three of them sought each other out at Lake Placid, drank a toast to me, and formed lasting relationships, and were also engaged in joint Rotary projects.

Display of the Rotary Four-Way Test had once again worked its magic. As a footnote, Nelson got his pearl craftsmen to fix a pearl on my Past District Governor's lapel badge. It is a badge which I still wear on occasions with pride and affection, tinged with nostalgia.

THE FIRST AFRICAN ROTARIAN AND
THE FIRST AFRICAN DISTRTICT GOVERNOR

No retrospective on District 220 can be complete without mentioning the names of Rtn James Mbotela and Rtn Phan Ntende.

JAMES MBOTELA was invited to join the Mombasa Rotary Club in 1968 and thus became the first African Rotarian in Mombasa, perhaps in the District. He proved to be an excellent Rotarian. He was a teacher by profession, had gone on to be an officer in the Port Administration, and subsequently became an Executive Director of Nyali Ltd. He had excellent command of the English language and was a considerable raconteur. He would regularly regale visiting Rotarians with his stories of how he was descended from slaves and how his grandfather had been rescued from an Arab slave ship by the Royal Navy in the Indian Ocean and settled in Freretown near Mombasa. Apparently Freretown was named after Sir Bartlett Frere who was the naval captain who was responsible for freeing many slaves.

RTN PHAN NTENDE of Kampala has certainly earned himself a place in Rotary history by being the first ever African Governor of District 220. I had the pleasure of meeting him for the first time during my official visit to Kampala. He was reluctant to accept the nomination for District Governor, because I believe he had political ambitions in Uganda. He was certainly one of the most popular individuals I have ever come across. He was finally cajoled into accepting the nomination at my District Conference in Mauritius.

I believe his becoming a District Governor in 1971/72 was one of the best things that happened to Rotary in East and Central Africa. It also proved to all that, regardless of race, any Rotarian could make it to the highest office in the District, so long as he had the right credentials. I would like to believe that the present prosperity of Rotary in Uganda is due in no small measure to his governorship.

*His Highness addressing the Mombasa Rotary
Club Lunch at the Oceanic Hotel 1961.
(Third from left: Mrs. Dolatkhanu Badrudin
Kanji, His Highness, President Badrudin
Alibhai Kanji, Mr Foster, Countess Roshan
Dhala and Ken Adcock)*

*Presenting Margaret
Mbotela, wife of First
African Rotarian, to
HH The Aga Khan
at Rotary Lunch at
the Oceanic Hotel,
Mombasa – 1961.*

*Picture shows me
presenting a banner to
Phan Ntende after his
election as the District
Governor Nominee. The
banner proclaims that the
Kampala Rotary Club
was now the home of the
DG Nominee.*

Rotary: as I Look Back

I settled in London in 1973. My initial business in London was a little grocery business called Whiteman's Dairy in Holland Street, off Kensington Church Street. I was on leave of absence from the Mombasa Rotary Club.

One of our customers was Dimpy Brown whose husband Jack had an office directly opposite the shop. She told Jack that the new Indian owner of the shop was wearing a Rotary badge on his blue overall. Jack was a Past President of the Kensington Rotary Club and was curious about me. He dropped in and invited me to come along to the Kensington Club, which used to meet then at the Bailey's Hotel in South Kensington.

I had visited the club several times as Jack's guest when the President, Selwyn Place suggested I should join the club. So I joined in 1973. I believe I am the first Indian to belong the Kensington Club. I am now a Senior Active member and a Past President of the Kensington Rotary Club. Having belonged to the Kensington Club since 1973, I am one of the two oldest surviving members of the club.

I often look back on my fifty years in Rotary. It has done much to influence and enrich my life, and has certainly made a most powerful impact. I was a Rotarian before I married Zeenat. One joins Rotary for what one can put into Rotary and not what one can get out of Rotary. But Rotary has done so much for me. It has given me so much. I don't know what I can do to repay this awesome debt. I have partially repaid this debt by introducing at least two outstanding fellows to Rotary.

First was Pip Barnes whom I proposed for membership in 1971 in Mombasa who went on to become a District Governor of my old District. The second is Rtn Bashir Chatoo, who was introduced to me by Hakim Adamjee. Bashir joined the Kensington Rotary Club in 1974/1975, went on to become the President and continues to be a popular and respected member of the club. In turn, he has introduced new members to Kensington who continue to make their contributions. And so Rotary continues.

I have been a Rotarian for over half a century, and have been privileged to serve in many different capacities, on two different continents. I have visited some seventy-five different Rotary clubs all over the world, and have probably addressed around fifty. I can now stand back and take a detached look at Rotary. There is much I can praise. There are one or two things I could comment upon.

Rotary, of course, is a Service organisation. Broadly speaking, Rotary channels its service through four avenues of service.

First is Club Service which exemplifies the first Object of Rotary, which is the development of acquaintance as an opportunity for service.

Second is Vocational Service which deals with the second Object of Rotary which is to do with high ethical standards in business and professions, the recognition of the worthiness of all useful occupations and the dignifying of each Rotarian's occupation as an opportunity to serve society.

Then there is Community Service which, in keeping with the third Object of Rotary, encourages the application of the ideal of service in each Rotarian's personal, business and community life.

The last is International Service, which is consonant with the fourth Object of Rotary, which is the advancement of international understanding, goodwill and peace through a world fellowship of business and professional persons united in the ideal of service.

In my visits to Rotary clubs throughout the world, I found that every club struggled with the second Object of Rotary, the one that deals with Rotary's vocational aspirations. This is not really surprising. This ideal was first enunciated during a time when Rotarians were all self-employed, independent shop owners, professionals and the like. They were more in charge of their destinies than we are today. They could, if they wanted to, ensure that their shops and offices and surgeries and so on, could practice high ethical standards and use their vocations as an opportunity to serve society.

Today, just about everybody is an employee, or is at least answerable to investors or Boards of Directors. Any personal aspirations for high ethical standards are subservient to the need for profitability. We now live in an age where the "bottom line" is tops and everybody wants a "bigger bang for his buck". Even schools and hospitals have to show profit or at least break even. It is common practice for businesses and institutions to publish their Mission Statements. Few of them frankly admit what their first Mission is. Reconciling the need for profitability with Rotary's vocational aspiration is a tall order indeed.

My biggest personal disappointment is that Rotary is generally perceived as a community service and fund raising organisation. This perception is perhaps perpetuated by Rotarians themselves who seem to judge the performance of their club by the number and size of their community service projects.

I do not decry community service – not at all. I feel, however, that the special opportunity that Rotary provides is the opportunity for advancing the cause of international understanding goodwill and peace. Membership in an international body like Rotary opens windows and doors. We must learn to look out through those windows and venture out through those doors if we wish to make the most of the opportunity which is ours as members of a truly international organisation.

The Lohana Connection

Meeting Hasmukhbhai Mehta

My Version of Lohana History

Meeting
Hasmukhbhai Mehta

Speak to any Ismaili whose forefathers hail from the Indian sub-continent, and they would probably say that their forefathers were Lohanas before they became Ismailis. I myself have always been vaguely aware of this without thinking too much about it. That is, until I happened to meet Hasmukhbhai Mehta. Hasmukhbhai, is a prominent Bombay industrialist, and a member of the Bombay Rotary Club.

He was a regular visitor to London in the nineteen-eighties. He was always accompanied by his wife Devi Bahen and his two charming daughters Rupa and Manisha, and they normally stayed in an apartment in Kensington. It was my good fortune to meet him at the Kensington Rotary Club one afternoon, back in 1983. He was a keen Rotarian and made up his attendance whenever he travelled. We happened to sit next to each other at lunch and we engaged in conversation. I figured that anybody called Hasmukh Mehta must speak Gujarati, and accordingly I addressed him in Gujarati. I think he was chuffed at finding a fellow-Rotarian in London who liked to talk in Gujarati.

He was interested in what I was doing in London. I told him that I was the Managing Director of a company which owned and operated hotels. He actually visited both the Swiss Cottage Hotel in London and the Oatlands Park Hotel in Weybridge. We met regularly in between and on one occasion in 1987 when our family went to Bombay to attend Quassim Cassams' marriage to Charoo Shahane. The Mehta family was incredibly warm and hospitable. Last year, that is, in 2006, accompanied by Shariffa and Yusuf Keshavjee, and Sultan and Amir Cassam, Zeenat and I were privileged to attend Hasmukhbhai and Devi Bahen's 50th Wedding Anniversary celebrations at their home in Juhu in Bombay.

Hasmukhbhai is a great conversationalist, with a keen sense of history, and is versed in the Vedas. His conversation is usually liberally sprinkled with Sanskrit quotations. And he is a great family man. He once asked me if I knew where my ancestors came from. I told him that I believed that my forefathers were Lohanas, who became Ismaili Muslims in the dim and distant past. I knew that we were Kathiawadis, because our mother tongue was Gujarati. I also had a copy of my grandfather's Will wherein he describes himself as "I, Janmohamed Hasham of Junagadh State in India". He asked me if I knew anything about the Lohana community. The answer was that I had friends amongst the Lohana community but did not have any historical knowledge.

Hasmukhbhai gave me a potted history of the Lohanas and how numbers of Lohanas happened to convert to the Ismaili faith. He clarified that what he was telling me was folk-lore and had been handed down verbally from one generation to the next. He certainly aroused my interest in the subject. I started talking to people who might know. And I also read newspaper and magazine articles on the subject, mostly in Gujarati. Based on what

Hasmukhbhai Mehta (on the left) and Ajit Shahane of Pune, India, in animated conversation in the lounge of the Oatlands Park Hotel during their visit to London circa 1987.

I have gleaned in my random searches, I have put together a frankly romantic "history" of what might have happened. However, my story has more than a mere grain of truth in it and is perhaps not to be totally discarded as a figment of imagination or as an exercise in wishful thinking.

Hasmukhbhai, in the middle at his 50th wedding anniversary party in Mumbai 2006, and in picture below Anup Jalota who regaled guests with brilliant Hindi and Gujarati songs, at the party with his wife.

MY VERSION OF LOHANA HISTORY

It has been suggested that Lohana roots may be traced back to approximately 500 to 250 years BC, to the times of Lord Rama – and that the Lohanas are followers of Shree Ram Chandra and Sita through their son Lava, pronounced "love".

Legend has it, that, under pressure from the people of the city state of Ayodhya, and due to intrigue within the Palace, Shree Ram had felt obliged to send his pregnant wife Sita into exile. Sita took refuge in the ashram of Shree Valmiki, sage and poet. That place is believed to be called Ram Tirath, not far from present day Amritsar. According to ancient Punjabi tradition, her twin sons Lava and Kush were born in Punjab, and in latter years, the City of Kasur was founded by Kush and Lahore by Lava.

When the twin brothers Lava and Kush grew up they learnt of the grave injustice which had been done to their mother. Legend has it that they raised an army and were prepared to wage a war against their father, but were eventually reconciled with him.

Lohanas are said to be descendants of Lava, and apparently were one of the eighteen Kshatriya (warrior) tribes called Lavan, and one theory is that the name Lohana is a corruption of the word of Lavan.

Another school of thought believes that the name Lohana is a composite of two words. The first word is "Loh" which means iron, and the second word is "Rana" which means a warrior, or a soldier. Hence a Loharana, or a Lohana, is a soldier strong as iron. According to this belief, they used to live in the 10th or the 11th century in a region called "Lohar Pradesh", which was made up of what are now parts of modern day Afghanistan, Pakistan,

Kashmir and the Hindu Kush regions. Being in the Northwest corner of the Indian sub-continent, they frequently did battle with Turkish and other foreign invaders, which further consolidated their reputation as fearless warriors and leaders.

It has been recorded that the Lohanas were a prominent community of the Kshatriya caste that originated in the Northwest of India. They then settled in Sindh. They migrated yet once more in the early thirteenth century. It is said that they left Sindh because they felt that their identity was increasingly threatened in Sindh and other northern provinces. They began to migrate towards Kutch, Saurashtra and Gujarat. (See map). The Gujaratis were a peaceable people and welcomed the Lohanas with open arms.

There was neither need nor opportunity for the Lohanas to practice their martial skills and prowess in Gujarat, and gradually many Lohanas took to trade and business. Thus the once-proud warriors of the Kshatriya caste gradually became involved in activities which were more associated with the Vaishyas who were lower in the caste system pecking order. It was literally a case of swords being turned into ploughshares.

(For the benefit of those not familiar with the Indian caste system, there were four major castes: Brahmins who were scholars and priests; Kshatriyas who were rulers and warriors; Vaishyas who were the traders; and Shudhras who were farmers and artisans. There was yet another group of people who did the most menial jobs, and they were called the "untouchables", now referred to as Dalits.)

Hasmukhbhai pointed out to me that Lohanas are distinguishable from the natives of Gujarat. As northerners who came from mountainous regions they were of bigger build and were of fairer complexion. According to Hasmukhbhai, even to this day, many descendants of the original Lohanas (including Ismailis) bear traces of their racial heritage. However due to inter-marriage over the years with other peoples in Gujarat, these characteristics are now becoming less pronounced.

Lohanas are credited with great achievements. It has been suggested that the father of the founder of the Sikh religion, was a Loharana named Kalidas Chandarana. Guru Nanak Devji took the name of Bedi as his family name later. The father of the creator of Pakistan, Mohamedali Jinnah, was a Lohana. His name was Jinabhai Thakkar. Swami Gnanjivandas later known as Yogiji Maharaj, leader of the Swaminarayan faith, was of Lohana origin. Other famous leaders of Lohana stock include Saint Shri Jalaram, Bhikshu Akhand Anand, Thakkar Bapa, Shree Nanjibhai Kalidas Mehta, the Madhvanis and Dada Jasraj, amongst many others. It has been suggested that the Gujarati Lohanas, the Khojas, the Memons, the Lohar Sikhs and even the Pakhtuns were of the same stock.

According to Hasmukhbhai, The Ismaili Pirs (Missionaries) came to India from Iran from the thirteenth century onwards. They came to India to spread the Ismaili faith. Hasmukhbhai is of the opinion that the Pirs found members of the Lohana community more receptive to their teachings. This was probably due to the fact that Lohanas were relative newcomers to Gujarat so their roots were not as deep as the other communities. Lohanas who were converted to Islam are known as Khojas. Many of them retain their Hindu names. I belong to an Ismaili Khoja family. My great great grandfather's name was Verjee son of Shivji whose father was Haji. All tese are Hindu names, with the exception of Haji perhaps.

Research by modern scholars seems to support the above theory. It is generally accepted that the Ismaili faith was introduced into that part of the Indian subcontinent in the fourteenth century. There is interesting research on the subject contained in the Encyclopaedia of Modern Asia, "Ismaili Communities – South Asia", by Farhad Daftari and Azim Nanji, of the Institute of Ismaili Studies.

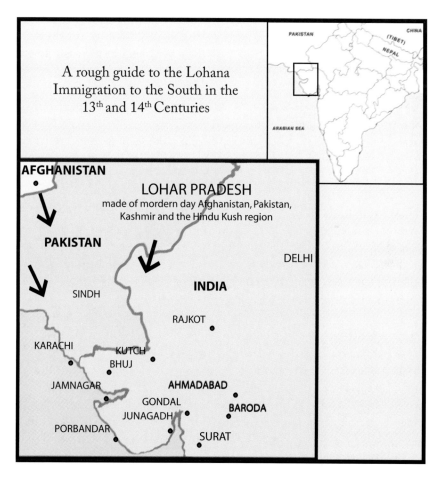

I am fairly convinced that my forefathers were converted during that period or thereafter. Whilst it cannot be conclusive in itself, it is interesting to note that my great great grandfather Verjee was the first member of our family to give Muslim names to his children. His six sons were named Mussa, Hasham (my great grandfather), Suleman,

Jiwa, Ali and Pirmohamed.

Whilst I am resigned to not being able to establish exactly when my ancestors became Ismailis, a tantalising thought will always linger in my mind. Did any of my ancestors actually get to meet any of the Ismaili Pirs who came from Persia, and who convinced them to embrace the Ismaili faith. Today, after so many centuries, Ismailis of Indian origin continue to relate to the Pirs, like Pir Sadardin and Pir Hasan Kabirdin and Pir Shamsh amongst others. This is because of the heritage of Ginans they have left behind. In common with so many others, I too have a passion for the wonderful Ginans which they composed and set to such beautiful ragas. I continue to recite them with awe and wonderment, for the wisdom they contain is as relevant today as it was in the 13th and 14th centuries.

IN MEMORIAM

IN MEMORIAM
Inna Lillahi Wa Inna Ilahi Raji'un

A quote from my Collection of Cynical Wisdom states; "Men age better than women. On the other hand they die sooner". This of course is a comment born out of cynicism, and would probably have been more facetious in origin than anything else. However, as I reflect on my own life and the number of people – my contemporaries, relatives, friends, associates – who have died, many so prematurely, during my lifetime, it becomes evident that there is more truth in this cynical comment than one may at first credit.

I have tried to recall those who have impacted my life, and many of whom have died well before they should have, and I discover that the number of men who have died far exceeds the number of women. To quote from William Shakespeare in "As You Like It", "All the world is a stage, and all the men and women merely players; they have their exits and entrances, and one man in his time plays many parts..."

My list of departed friends shows that far too many male actors have exited the stage of life earlier than female ones – the disparity is unbelievably disproportionate. Nonetheless, many female actors also die too young. And so, I list below, in no particular order, the girls who impacted upon my life, and who died too soon:

MUNIRA, nee Jindani, my first wife, who passed away in 1974 at the age of forty-one.

Munira and myself on board the french liner "Pierre Loti" when we sailed back from Eourope via Suez in 1955.

Munira with my sister Sultan and her husband Amir Cassam. We collected the Opel Kapitan from the factory in Russelsheim in Germany. We toured Germany, Austria, Switzerland, France, Holland, Belgum, England and Scotalnd. After the holiday Munira and I drove to Marseilles and boarded the "Pierre Loti" and also brought the car back to Mombasa.

ASHRAF, Daughter of Janu Kaka and Malek Kaki, my friend and neighbour in Mombasa, who died in the tragic Likoni Ferry accident of 1950.

SHIRIN (Shilo), My lovely cousin, Ebrahim Mama's daughter, married to Amir R. Kassim-Lakha, who died of a heart condition in early 1970s.

My cousin SHIRIN, Bhanifai's daughter, vivacious and charming, who succumbed to illness at an early age.

GULSHAN VERJEE, Founder member of Lido Club and daughter of Jenafai and Hassanali Kaka, dear family friends of long standing.

GULZAR Satchu, Dearest friend, sadly taken away at an early age. Picture below was taken in 1969 when she was the President of the Inner Wheel Club of Mombasa. She is flanked on either side by myself as the Governor of Rotary International District 220, and Jagdish Sondhi, Director of Lions International. Mansur Satchu was the President of the Mombasa Rotary Club in the same year.

And sadly, so many male friends, relatives, and associates, who impacted upon and enriched my life in so many different ways – many of whom were snatched away at early ages. Once again, in no particular order:

My father KASSAM JANMOHAMED who died in 1950. I never remember him as a "young" man although he was only 45 when he died.

*Left to right: Late **Amir P Dhanji**, Late **Gulshan Verjee**, and far right, Late **Abdul Valli**.*

163

ABDUL VALLI, One of the founder members of the Lido Club. So full of life. We had identical cars, the first two-tone Zephyr Zodiacs to come to Kenya. His always looked brighter, for his family owned the White Hart Petrol Station on Kilindini Road.

AMIR PREMJI DHANJI, Another founder member of the Lido Club, debonair, full of beans, car enthusiast and keen badminton player.

MOHAMEDALI JADAVJI KHOJA, Married to my cousin Shirin Hussein Janmohamed. Probably the first marriage between a South African and an East African Ismaili. Died tragically in a fire in Louis-Trichardt in South Africa. They made such a handsome couple.

NOORALI VALLI RAHEMTULLAH, Noorali was some years ahead of me in the Aga Khan School. His was the first funeral I had to officiate at as the new Kamadia of the Mombasa Jamat Khana in 1962.

BADRU EBOO, Eldest son of Sir Eboo Pirbhai. Dearest friend and founder of the Pomegranate Club in Nairobi. We shared common interests and had wonderful times in Kenya and London. Master of Ceremonies and life and soul of every party.

There was always laughter when Badru Eboo was around. Above picture was taken around 1971/1972 at the newly built Hilton Hotel in Nairobi at an Embassy party Standing from left to right: Noor Eboo, myself, the Ambassador's wife, Badru, Zarin Eboo and Zeenat.

SULTANALI JANMOHAMED CASSAM. (on the right) Cousin and dear friend. We used to be members of the Navnat Vanik Mahahjan and had so many picnics in Bamburi using the pick-up from Harvey's Butchery. Our mutual friend Gulab on the left.

BADRUDIN HUSSEIN SULEMAN DAMJI, Known as Badru Mama to all, but my real Mama. He was my father's friend, and then equally mine. Badrudin's Sports House, which I ran for so many years, was started by him.

Above picture was taken at our beach house in Bamburi in 1951, a year after my father passed away. From left to right; Badru Mama, Hassanali Kaka, Sultanali Hussein Janmohamed (Dudio), Dr. Mohamedali Rana, Mr. Habib Keshavjee, myself and Fatehali Hassanali Mussa Jetha (Fatlo). As I write this in September 2007, I realise that out of the seven persons in the photo, I am the only one who is alive today.

FATEHALI HASSANALI MUSSA JETHA (In the middle). Dear friend and companion. Here witnessing Princess Margaret Aly Khan autographing her photo I had taken in 1951. Picture below:

AMIN DHALA,
Another dear friend
of many years.
Called away too
soon. A good man,
if ever there was one.
Remembered as a
gentle man as well as
gentleman.

*We are seen here after a
sleepover in Bamburi*

SADRUDIN ABDULLA ALIBHAI KANJI, Good friend, Structural Engineer by profession. He was married to Guli Fatehali, sitting on his right.

UMEDALI GOKAL LADHA, My brother-in-law and partner in Whiteman's Dairy in Holland Street. We used to work eleven hours a day, six and a half days a week.

*I took this picture outside our beach house in Bamburi, north of Mombasa in 1967. From left to right: Amir Cassam, Francis (in the background), "Moto" Quassim, **Umed**, Sultan, Azmeena, my mother Rabhia, "Nano" Quassim, Roshan, Zeenat.*

ABDUL RAMZAN JAMAL, only son of Ramzan Jamal. Zeenat and I brought him from Kenya in 1961 to enrol him at Mill Field School in Somerset. He died in 1967 at the age of eighteen.

Photo on the Serpentine in the Hyde Park shows my cousin Haydar Bhanji, Zeenat and young Abdul.

NURDIN NANJI (Right of picture) With myself, Nurali Sayani,
Hakim Adamjee and Lord Amir Bhatia.

ARUN PATEL, Another lovely chap of my generation from Mombasa. Soft spoken and
genuine individual. Occupant of Penthouse atop Ambalal House. The landmark building
was named after his father Hon. A. B. Patel.

KISHU HIRA,
Young and
irrepressible fellow-
Rotarian friend, who
lived life to the hilt.

AMIR JAMAL, Zeenat's uncle. We were both born in Kisumu around the
same time. We were colleagues in Oatlands Investments.

ABDUL NAZERALI,
Friend, solicitor,
adviser, and often
partner, in projects
in UK.

SADRU KASSAM SULEMAN DAMJI, youngest brother of Rajabali and Jimmy Damji. Always brought a smile to my face. Picture taken in Vancouver in 2000 shows from left to right **Sadru Damj**i, Amala Prinja, Prem Prinja, Roshan Verjee, myself, Gulshan Damji and our host Mansur Verjee. H.E. Prem Pinja is the Consul General for Kenya in the UAE.

SHABUDIN ALIBHAI RAHIM, My class-mate for many years at the Aga Khan High in Mombasa. We were intense rivals and were always chosen to lead opposing teams in school debates, both in Gujarati and English.

JIMMY RAHIM, Shabudin's younger brother and also our class-mate. An ace table tennis and hockey player, and had a physique which was the envy of most boys in our class. My friend and neighbour in St. John's Avenue for many years.

*At "Virgo" Birthday Party in Maidenhead 1996. Left to right Zeenat, Badru Alibhai, Zeiny Hirji, Aziz Dhanji, Mary Shamji and **Jimmy Rahim**.*

UMEDALI SOMJI died in 1971 whilst holding office of Mukhi Saheb of Kuze Jamat Khana in Mombasa.

Picture shows the two of us at the Imamat day ceremony in Mombasa in 1970.

KASSAMALI MANJI JANMOHAMED, Probably my all-time favourite cousin in the 1940s. JOHN MANJI JANMOHAMED, Kassamali's younger brother.

FOURTEEN FALLS - 1951 From left to right: Myself, Kassamali Manji Janmohamed, Fareeda, Sultanali Hussein Janmohamed (Dudio), Fatehali Manji Janmohamed and John Manji Janmohamed.

HAIDER JIVRAJ MAHERALI, Handsome and dashing badminton player from Nairobi and my rival in more ways than one. I was his Best Man when he married Zeitun Satchu in Mombasa.

WILFRID ARTHUR BARNES (PIP), I introduced him into Rotary. He went on to become a District Governor. Hon Swedish Consul. We drove to Rotary conference in Lusaka in 1972 via Tanga, Dodoma, Iringa, Mbeya, Kipiri Mposhi and into Zambia.

MEHNDI LALANI, Friend and businessman. First of my friends to travel to the Far East.

DR SHAMSUDDIN (MILLER) SOMJI, friend and doctor. Doyen of Mombasa's medical fraternity. Photo in London, 1987.

AMIR KASSAM, A friendly in-law. (His mother Fatma and I were first cousins).
Lover of life and bon viveur.

Photo shows the two of us the day his daughter Nazira and my son Quassim got married in 1979.

Quassim and Nazira take their very first steps in matrimonial harness, supervised by my mother Rabhia.

HAKIM ADAMJEE, dearest friend and like a brother since 1939. His death leaves an unfilled void.

*Rustam Hira Birthday Party 1939. Left to right: myself, **Hakim Adamjee**, Rustam Hira, Anver Jivanjee, Dinoo Merwanji.*

We organised a Re-union sixty years later in 1999, at the Oatlands Park Hotel in Weybridge, Surrey, England.

Picture shows myself, Hakim, Anver and Rustam. Zeenat and Pushpa Hira seated. Fizza Adamjee and Sarah Jivanjee could not make it. Sadly, we have lost contact with Dinoo Merwanjee.

MADHAV KARVE, dear friend, respected Physician, bridge companion of many years. Golfer and tennis player. Rememberd for his great sense of humour.

Picture shows from left to right Zarin Gulamani, MADHAV KARVE, Hema Karve, Sadru Gulamani and Zeenat. I took the photo outside the Royal Hotel in Weston-Super-Mare in 1988. My father and his cousins were at college in this town 65 years ago.

JOHN KANJI, we worked together in the Diamond Trust Board in Kenya and then started Uftonridge and Wolverburgh properties in London.

Ex-directors Re-union 1985 at Swiss Cottage Hotel, London. From left to right: myself, **John Kanji,** *Ameer Somji, Zul Nimji, Noorali Sayani and Shiraz Maherali.*

PICTORIAL MEMORIES

Six Ismaili Council Presidents of Kenya at a quarterly meeting in Mombasa 1971.

Front Row: Akbar Nanji (Kenya Council), Count Fatehali Dhala (Executive Council), Diwan Sir Eboo Pirbhai (Supreme Council) Back Row: Mohamedali Rajan Lalji (Nairobi Council), Ameer Janmohamed (Mombasa Council) & Malek Valimohamed (Kisumu Council).

Receiving the District Governor 1947. Port Reitz Airport - Mombasa

Mombasa Rotarians receive District Governor Rtn. D. G. Gerard A. Leyds of Johannesburg. From left to right: Rtn. Felix Dias (Hon. Portuguese Consul), Rtn. R. D. Doshi, Rtn. Anant Pandya, Rtn. R. A. Hawkins, District Governor Gerard A. Leyds, unidentified Rotarian, and Rtn. Kassam Janmohamed.

His Highness Prince Aly Khan, who was also a Major
in the British Army, periodically visited Kenya.
He honoured our family by visiting the Regal in 1942.
It was an occasion
for our families and other leaders of the community to pose
for this historical photo.
In 1958 he further honoured our family by very kindly
laying the foundation stone of
the new City House (pictures in page 190) in Mombasa.

Middle row: Kassam Janmohamed, Prince Aly Khan, Mrs. Panbai Janmohamed Hasham &
Mrs. Sikinabai Dhala Visram Sitting on the floor: Roshan KJ, Malek HJ, Ameer KJ, Sultan
KJ, Sultanali HJ & Noor HJ. Standing: Major Lutufali Maherali, Mrs. Mohamedali Dhala,
Vazier Kassam Khimji, Varasiani Zerabai Fatehali Dhala, Vazier Fatehali Dhala, Dolu HJ,
Shirin HJ, Prince Abdulla, Guli HJ, my mother Rabhiabai, Akber Jamal Gangji (Married to
Dolu HJ), Shamsudin HJ, Hussein Janmohamed, Mr. Vithalani, Mr Odhavjibhai Anandji.

Prince Aly Khan visits the offices of The Jubilee Insurance Co. Ltd., on Kilindini Road, Mombasa, 25th. February 1939.

Standing from left to right: Mr. Valli Rahemtulla, Mr. Abdulla Hasham Gangji, Mr. Hussein Janmohamed, Mr. Kassamali Paroo, H.S.H. Prince Aly Khan, Count G. M. N. Jindani, Mr Fatehali Dhala, Premji Dhanji, Mr. Alibhai Kassam Lakha, Vazier Kassam Khimji, Prince Abdullah and the General Manager Mr. S. R. Idgunji.

Sultan Mohamed Shah Aga Khan visits offices of the Jubilee Insurance Co. Ltd. On corner of Fort Jesus Road and Mvita Road, Mombasa.   Circa 1945.

Sitting from left to right: Sir Eboo Pirbhai, Mr. Hassan Kassam Lakha, Mr. Abdulla Hasham Gangji, Count Jindani, Mowlana Sultan Mohamed Shah, Mr. Kassamali Paroo (Managing Director), Mr. Fatehali Dhala, Mr. Kassam Janmohamed & Mr. Dhanji Jadavji Bhatia. Standing first row L. to R.: Mr. Ismail Valli Jamal, Mr Salehmohamed Ladha, Mr. Dhanji Manji, Mr. Lalji Mangalji, Mr. Alibhai Kassam Lakha, Mr. Premji Dhanji, Mr. Valli Rahemtulla, Mr. Kassam Suleman Damji, & Mr. Shamsudin Tejpar. Second row L. to R. :1-Itmadali Shivji Nurmohamed, 2-Badru Mussani, 3- Abdul Nurmohamed Dossa, 5-Rajan Jamal Mullani, 7-Shabudin Hasham Amarshi.

**London
1927\1928**

*My father with his younger sister Fatma and her husband Count Jindani in Europe around
1927/1928. The cut of my father's suit seems to suggest that he was on a student's budget.
Count Jindani, on the other hand, clearly patronised an altogether better class of tailor.
By this time Count Jindani was already a confidante of Sultan Mohamed Shah, President
of the Executive Council based in Zanzibar, and was a frequent visitor to Europe.*

Fatma Fui was a polished young lady, much travelled, spoke excellent English, hobnobbed
with the families of the Sultan of Zanzibar and the British Resident of Zanzibar, and had
the reputation of being an excellent Bridge player. She was an elegant lady and carried
herself with considerable haughtiness. She was always attired in the traditional Ismaili
attire of long frock and pacchhedi.

*1948 Picture
shows her with my
mother and Jenabai
Hassanalli Hussein
Suleman Verjee.
I have quoted
frequently from the
diary of her husband
Hassanalli Hussein
Suleman Verjee*

1966 Cricket match between Aga Khan Club and Aga Khan Council. Left to right: Abdul (Baboo) Hirji, Mohamed Abdalla, Ameer Janmohamed, Amir Somji and Mohamedali Rashid.

Cricket match between the Rotary Club and the Lions Club of Mombasa, played at the Coast Stragglers cricket ground, Mombasa 1967.

Standing from left to right:: -?-, Arthur Ratcliffe, Sadruddin Abdullah Alibhai Kanji, -?-, Mike Wood, Aziz Kassim-Lakha, Yusuf Mamujee, Madhav Karve, Dhiroo Shah (Lions Club President), Manu Chandaria, Homi Burjorjee (Rotary Club President), Ameer Janmohamed, -?-, Amir Paroo, -?-, Percy Coulter, Sadiq Ghalia, Rajni Shah. Sitting from left to right: Baldev Wadhvani, Shamsher Dhillon, Rasik Patel, -?-, Sadru Jaffer, Mansur Satchu, -?-.

THE JUBILEE SWIMMING CLUB

THE JUBILEE SWIMMING CLUB HAS BEEN IN EXISTENCE SINCE A LONG TIME. MEMBERS OF THE CLUB WOULD DRIVE UP TO THE OLD PORT AT SIX O'CLOCK EVERY MORNING AND WOULD BE ROWED ACROSS NEAR THE OPPOSITE SHORE WHERE THEY WOULD SWIM IN THE DEEP CLEAR WATERS OF THE CHANNEL. ON OCCASIONS THEY WOULD ACTUALLY LAND ON THE OPPOSITE SHORE, WHERE THIS PICTURE WAS TAKEN. LEADING MEMBERS OF THE COMMUNITY USED TO TAKE PART IN THE CLUB'S ACTIVITIES AS EVIDENCED BY THIS PHOTO. I CONTINUED TO BELONG TO THE CLUB UNTIL MID NINETEEN SIXTIES AND BELONG TO THAT EXCLUSIVE BAND OF SWIMMERS WHO HAD CROSSED THE CHANNEL

A2- Shamsu Mohamed Jamal. A4- Sultan Husein Rajan. A6- Amir Hassan Juma. A9-Rajan Kachra & Jafferali K.S.Meghji. A-10 Badru Kara Kanji. A11- (?) Maherali. A12-Badrudin Hussein Suleman Damji. A13-Ramzan Lakdawalla & Husein Habib Kara. A15-Nurali Salehmohamed. A16- Fatehali Dhala. A17-Husein Janmohamed. A18-Husein Vellani. A19-Hirji Mawji & Kassam Suleman Damji. A20-Badru Mussa Ladha. A21-Fazal Raghavji. A22-Ramzan Husein Meghji Dossa. A23-Shamsu Lakhoo. A24-Mussa Dawood. A25-Ismail Janmohamed. A26-Maherali Ramji & Jamal Manji Rahemtulla. A28-Kanji Karsan. A29-Mohamedali Paroo. A30-Gulamhusein Tejpar.

MOMBASA. CIRCA 1938/1939.

BOTH WAYS ON THE SAME DAY. OUR TEACHER AND LIFE-GUARD WAS A CHAP CALLED SAIDI AND THE VERY OLD BOATMAN WAS CALLED SENGAY. OTHER HEALTH CONSCIOUS INDIAN COMMUNITIES ALSO HAD THEIR OWN BOATS AND IT WAS NOT UNUSUAL TO FIND A HUNDRED PLUS PEOPLE OF DIFFERENT INDIAN COMMUNITIES SWIMMING TOGETHER EACH MORNING TAKING INVIGORATING EXERCISE IN THE COOL WATERS OF THE INDIAN OCEAN. THE BOATS WOULD RETURN TO THE MOMBASA SIDE OF THE CHANNEL BY SEVEN A.M. EACH MORNING. I HAVE TRIED TO CREATE A GRID IN AN ATTEMPT TO FACILITATE IDENTIFICATION OF VARIOUS PEOPLE IN THE PHOTO. MY APOLOGIES TO THE NUMBER OF PEOPLE WHOM I HAVE FAILED TO IDENTIFY. (I MYSELF AM AT D18).

A
B
C
D

8-19-20-21-22-23-24-25 -26-27-28-29-30-31

B9-Kassam Ramji. B10- (?) Jadavjee. B15-Zavahir Zaver Alibhai & Najmudin Hassan Juma. B18-Shamsu Chagan Nathoo. B20-Ebrahim Esmail Janmohamed. B21-Kassamali Tarmohamed. B23- Hassanali Boghani. B24-Hassanali Raghavjee. B26- Jafferali Boghani. B28-Hirji Kanji. B29- Mohamedali Nurani. B31-Abdul H. Kaloo. C2-Nazerali Dawood. C5-Husein Ramji. D6-Tajdin Chatur Virji. C8- (?) Bhagat. D12-Jimmy Damji. D14-Rajabali K.S.Damji. D15-Sadru Damji. D16-Chatur Virji. D17-Sultanali Husein Janmohamed & Sultan Hirji Kanji. D18-Ameer Janmohamed. D19-Abdulshamsh Husein Dhala. D24-Khatun Damji. D25-Mohamedali Merali Ramji. D29-Pyarali Hasan Juma and (?) Hirji Mawji.

July 1968 – at reception held by the Ismaili Community of Mombasa, Kenya At The Oceanic Hotel In Honour of Dr. Syyedna Mohamed Burhanuddin Saheb, spiritual leader of the Bohra Community.

1968 – at the wedding of James Mbotela to Margaret. On the steps of the Mombasa Memorial Cathedral, Mombasa. James was the first african member of the Mombasa Rotary Club.

Khatoon Javer (Now Mrs. Jimmy Damji) And Ameer Janmohamed, 1949 Winners of the Najma Cup, Badminton Mixed Doubles Trophy Mombasa

A visit to the Petticoat Lane in East London 1960.

Left to right: Zeenat, Guli Fatehali Eboo & Zarin Badru Eboo. Mahmood F. Eboo and Ahmadali E. Eboo with lollipops.

At the Epsom Derby 1960

Annual District Conference of Rotary District 220
Held at Boname Hall, Le Reduit, Mauritius June 1970

June 1970 – Being welcomed to the Government House,
Port Louis, Mauritius, by the Governor General Sir Leonard Williams.

Participating countries: Kenya, Uganda, Tanzania, Malawi, Zambia, Madagscar, Mauritius, La-reunion & Comores. Held under the chairmanship of Rtn. District Governor Ameer Janmohamed of Mombasa, Kenya.

Welcoming the Prime Minister Of Mauritius Sir Seewoosagar Ramgoolam

Entering the Throne Room of the Government House, Port Louis, Mauritius, for the Formal Opening of the Conference. From left to right: the Governor General Of Mauritius Sir Leonard Williams, District Governor Ameer Janmohamed, Prime Minister Sir Seewoosagar Ramgoolam, R.I.president's Representative Cyril Coles.

City House
Mombasa, Kenya

The new City House was completed in 1958.
It replaced the old buildings previously occupied
by Motor Mart & Exchange, facing the church, and Wardles
Chemists on Kilindini Road. The property includes the old city
house on the same facing and the building consisting of shops and
apartments facing the Manor Hotel site & Customs.
New building was designed by architects M/s. Vamos and Lustman
and built by contractors M/s. Alibhai Kanji & Sons Ltd.
Mr. Jagdish Sondhi's firm were the structural engineers.
It was the first building in Mombasa
incorporating an arcade and a fountain
in the central courtyard;
hence the restaurant being named Fontanella.

The foundation stone was laid By H. H. Prince Aly Khan in 1957. Director Ameer Janmohamed welcomes His Highness and guests, giving a brief history of the development.

Picture shows from left to right: Mrs. Sanobar Rana, Prince Aly Khan, Count Jindani, Dr. Rana (behind me) and Mr. Ebrahim Ismail Nathoo... back row: Munira and Jenny Bhabhi, And Sikinafai on the extreme right of the photo.

A delighted Prince Aly Khan declares the foundation stone "Well and truly laid". Next to him are Count Jindani and Mr. Badru Alibhai Kanji whose firm had contracted to build the new City House. Behind Prince Saheb are Dr. Rana, Shamsudin Hussein Janmohamed, Jagdish Sondhi (with moustache), then Sultanali Hussein Janmohamed, and Hussein Habib Kara in the major's uniform.

THREE PICTURES OF EBRAHIM MAMA.

Picture shows Prince Karim Aga Khan and Prince Amyn Mohamed, leading the Jamat in Eid Namaaz prayers in Nairobi in 1945. From left to right: Young Mohamed Jindani, Sir Eboo Pirbhai, Count Jindani, Mukhi Nazerali Madatali Suleman Verjee and Kamadia Ebrahim Hussein Suleman Damji (Ebrahim Mama).

Picture shows Ebrahim Mama partnering Prince Aly Khan in men's doubles, playing on the tennis court at Sir Eboo's house. Prince Abdullah assisting to retrieve the balls.

Picture shows Ebrahim Mama as the captain of Aga Khan club tennis team which won the Trenn Cup Asian Tennis League Competition in 1947. 1st left Mohamedali Dharamshi. 3rd. from left: Rahemtullah K. S. Verjee, John Karmali, Ebrahim Mama, Hassan Rattanshi, and Abdul Tejpar on the far right.

THREE PICTURES OF RAMZAN HASHAM JAMAL.

Zeenat's parents Ramzan Hasham Jamal and Khatibai wedding portrait in 1935

Mr. Dhanji Jadavji Bhatia and Mr. Ramzan Hasham Jamal, good friends, show how the debonair young business tycoons used to dress in Mwanza, Tanganyka Circa 1936

Cairo 1959: *left to right- Gulzar Noorali, Gulam Keshavjee, Malik Kassim-lakha, Zeenat, Ebrahim Ismail Nathoo, Mrs. Khatibai Ramzan Jamal, Nick Kassam, Roshan Aman Talib, Pirbhai Bharwani, Bhachibai Tejpar, Mrs. Nathoo and Ramzan Jamal.*

LONDON 1934

THIS PICTURE WAS TAKEN IN LONDON IN 1934.
SEATED IN MIDDLE ROW FROM LEFT TO RIGHT: KASSAM SUNDERJI SAMJI, MRS. FATMA
JINDANI, SULTAN MOHAMED SHAH. BEGUM SAHEBA (WITH MEERA JINDANI ON HER LAP),
VARAS JINDANI AND RAJABALI KASSAM SULEMAN VERJEE.
STANDING FROM LEFT TO RIGHT: KASSAMALI RAJAN LALJI, ALIMOHAMED JESSA BHALOO,
VAZIER MOHAMED VARAS SALEH, MY FATHER KASSAM JANMOHAMED, BAHADURALI
KASSAM SULEMAN VERJEE, NURMOHAMED R. HUSSEIN, UNIDENTIFIED STUDENT,
RAHEMTULLAH HIRJI BHANJI AND HUSSEIN JESSA BHALOO.
(Rahemtullah Hirji Bhanji married an English lady after qualifying as a Doctor.
They are the parents of Sir Ben Kingsley),
SEATED ON THE GROUND FROM L. TO R. : GOVERALI G. A. SHARIFF, AL-NOOR KASSAM
(NICK), GULZAR JINDANI, AND SALEH MOHAMED SALEH. (KASSAM SUNDERJI SAMJI,
VARAS G. M. N. JINDANI AND RAJABALI KASSAM SULEMAN VERJEE
WERE IN LONDON AS A THREE-MAN DELEGATION TO MAKE REPRESENTATIONS
TO THE SECRETARY OF STATE FOR THE COLONIES.)
(Their grievance was the discrimination of Aga Khan Schools in East Africa where the British Government was giving
them lesser Grant-in-aid compared to other Government run schools for Asians.)

194

MARCH 1970 – Laying the foundation stone of Rotary sponsored Hostel For Spastic Patients at the Mengo Hospital in Kampala . Zeenat and Rtn. Phan Ntende in the background.

JULY 2004. Thirty-four years later, a nostalgic visit to the Mengo Hospital Cerebral Palsy Hostel in Kampala, Uganda.

Remembrance Day, 11th November 1981. Laying a wreath at The Kensington War Memorial on behalf of the Kensington Rotary Club.

Oatlands Park Hotel, Weybridge. Second from left: John Hannah, Ameer Janmohamed, Amanda Donahue & 'Tiny' Lister at the shooting of scenes for the film " Circus" in May 1999.

*With H.H. Prince
Sadruddin Aga Khan
at The Diamond
Jubilee Hall Mombasa,
Kenya, August 1968.*

*With H.H. Prince
Sadruddin Aga Khan
at Chateau Bellerive,
Geneva, July 1997.*

*As Mukhi and Mukhiani of Mombasa Chief Jamat Khana 1964 in
ceremonial robes (worn on special occasions).*

GLOSSARY
GUJARATI WORDS AND PHRASES
USED IN THIS BOOK

BHAJIA = Made of chick-pea, or gram, or lentil flour. Ingredients can include potato, onion, vegetable leaves etc. Also known as Pakora.

CHANDLO/TILAK = Red dot worn on the forehead as a sign that one is a Hindu.

CHHANTA = Sprinkling of holy water for forgiveness of sins.

GADDHA = An ass.

CHATNI = Grated coconut pickle, chilly hot, which richly complements Bhajias.

GANTHIA = Savoury snack made from chickpeas.

GINAN = Literally Wisdom or Knowledge. Ginans are devotional hymns. Written by various Ismaili Pirs and set to classical Indian ragas. Described as "Indo-Ismaili Religious Lyrics" by Aziz Esmail in his book "A Scent of Sandalwood". Also "Songs of Wisdom and Circles of Dance" by Tazim R. Kassam.

GUSAL = Ritual cleansing and purification of a body prior to burial.

JALEBI = Indian sweetmeat, made of Maida flour batter, shaped in concentric circles, fried in ghee etc. A must for birthdays, weddings and festivals.

JAMAT = Community or congregation.

JAMAT KHANA = Community Centre, congregation place with prayer hall.

JAMPU DIP = Continent of India.

KIKOI = Waist to toe wrap around sarong-like male attire, quite often with African motifs.

MITHAI = Sweetmeats.

MOTO = Big.

MUKHI & KAMADIA = Lay appointees who officiate at Jamati prayers, weddings and funerals.

MUSAFAR-KHANA = Stopover for travellers.

NANO = Small.

PACHHEDI = Long piece of cloth or material to be wrapped around shoulder and head.

Pachhedis frequently have elaborate borders sewn around the edges. Worn by ladies in conjunction with long frocks.

PIRS = Missionaries, teachers and authors of Ginans.

ROTLO = Type of Indian bread, made of Bajra or Juwar, circular in shape and cooked over a griddle.

ROJI/ROZEE = Karma or destiny.

TIFFIN = 3 or 4 circular steel or tin boxes with lids, one on top of other, held together by a frame with handle, ideal for transportation of food.

VEDAS = Ancient Hindu scriptures in Sanskrit.

NOTE: Indian names are simple to pronounce in Gujarati, which is a phonetic language. People spell them in many ways in English. For instance, one name which is popular in my family is variously spelt as Kassam, Kassim or Cassam, or Quassim. Up until the nineteen thirties it was common practice to give suffixes to most names. Male names would have 'ali' or 'ally' added to them. I choose to be known as Ameer, but many older documents refer to me as Ameerally. Hence we have Madatali, or Kassamally, and so on. Girls had the suffix 'Khanu' added to their names. Hence my sisters Roshan and Sultan are described as Roshan Khanu and Sultan Khanu in old passports. There are upwards of four hundred and fifty Indian names in this book. My apologies for spelling inconsistencies.

CHRONOLOGY

This chronology is an ambitious attempt to provide perspective to the history of my ancestors by juxtaposing events in their lives with events happening elsewhere in the world around the same time.

PERIOD	NAME	NARRATION
3000BC	SHREE KRISHNA	BHAGVAD GITA
1525BC	MOSES	HAZRAT MUSSA
628BC	ZARATHUSTRA	FOUNDER ZOROASTRANISM & PARSIISM
566BC	BUDDHA	TRIPITIKA
551BC	CONFUCIUS	
350BC	ARISTOTLE	
250BC	SHREE RAM CHANDRA RAMAYANA	
150BC	GREEK & ROMAN SHIPS TRADE WITH KERALA FOR SPICES AND FIRST JEWS SETTLE ININDIA	
3BC	BIRTH OF JESUS CHRIST - HAZRAT ISSA	
AD33	CRUCIFIXION OF CHRIST	
571/632	**MUHAMMAD**	**HAZRAT NABI SAHEB**
622	**START OF MUSLIM CALENDAR**	

632	GHADIR KHUMM	SHIA/SUNNY DIVERGENCE
632/661	**HAZRAT ALI BIN ABU TALIB**	**1ST. IMAM, born AD600**
661/680	IMAM HUSSEIN	2ND. IMAM
680/713	ZAYN-AL-ABDIN	3RD. IMAM
713/733	MUHAMMAD AL-BAKIR	4TH. IMAM
733/765	JAFFER SADIQ	5TH. IMAM born in MEDINA
765	ISMAILIS EMERGE AS SEPARATE ENTITY	
/775	IMAM ISMAIL	6TH. IMAM born in SALAMIYA
775/813	MOHAMED BIN ISMAIL	7TH. IMAM born in MEDINA
813/828	WAFI AHMAD	8TH. IMAM born in SALAMIA
828/840	TAQI MOHAMED	9TH. IMAM
840/881	RADI ABDULLAH	10TH. IMAM
881/934	MOHAMED AL-MAHDI	11TH. IMAM Fatimid Caliphate
934/946	QUAIM	12TH. IMAM born in SALAMIA
946/952	MANSUR	13TH. IMAM
..../975	IMAM AL-MUIZZ	14TH. IMAM CAIRO
975/996	AZIZ	15TH. IMAM

980/1037	IBN SINA (AVICENNA)	
996/1021	HAKIM	6TH.IMAM - CAIRO
1021/1036	ZAHIR	17TH. IMAM
1036/1095	MUSTAN SIRBILLAH	18TH.IMAM
1048/1122	OMAR KHAYYAM	RUBAIYYATS
1066	NORMANS INVADE BRITAIN	
1090/1124	HASAN BIN SABBAH	ALAMUT PERIOD
1094	ISMAILIS AND BOHORAS SEPARATE	
1095/1097	NIZARI	19TH. IMAM born in CAIRO
1099	CRUSADERS CAPTURE JERUSALEM	
1097/1136	HADI BIN NIZAR	20TH. IMAM EGYPT
1136/1157	IMAM MOHTADI	21ST. IMAM born in IRAN
1139	PORTUGAL BECOMES INDEPNEDENT FROM SPAIN	
1157/1162	IMAM KAHIR	22ND. IMAM
1162/1166	ALA ZIKRI SALAM	23RD. IMAM
1166/1210	ALA MUHAMMAD	24TH. IMAM (End of Fatimid Caliphate Egypt)
1189	KING RICHARD I	KING OF ENGLAND
1207/1273	MOWLANA RUMI	
1210/1221	JALALUDIN HASSAN	25TH. IMAM

1215	MAGNA CARTA SIGNED BY KING JOHN	
1221/1255	ALAUDIN MOHAMED	26TH. IMAM
1231	CAMBRIDGE UNIVERSITY FOUNDED	
1248	OXFORD UNIVERSITY CHARTERED	
1255/1257	RUKHNUDDIN KHURSA	27TH. IMAM
1254/1324	MARCO POLO TRAVELS SILK ROUTE TO CHINA	
1257/1310	SHAMSUDIN MOHAMED	28TH. IMAM
1290	JEWS EXPELLED FROM ENGLAND	

APPROXIMATE START OF LOHANA MIGRATION FROM NORTHWEST AREAS OF INDIA TO GUJARAT, KUTCH & KATHIAWAD VIA SINDH

| 1296 | SCOTLAND ANNEXED BY ENGLAND | |
| 1310/1370 | KASSIM SHAH | 29TH. IMAM |

APPROXIMATE COMMENCEMENT OF INTRODUCTION OF SHIA IMAMI ISMAILI FAITH TO PEOPLES OF GUJARAT, KUTCH AND KATHIAWAD

1300/1416	PIR SADRUDDIN	KHOJKI COMES INTO USE
1341	PIR HASSAN KABIRDIN, SON OF PIR SADRUDDIN BORN IN INDIA	
1362	ENGLISH BECOMES OFFICIAL LANGUAGE IN PARLIAMENT	

1370/1423	ISLAM SHAH	30TH. IMAM
1382	BIBLE TRANSLATED INTO ENGLISH FOR THE FIRST TIME	
1423/1463	MOHAMED BIN ISLAM SHAH	31ST. IMAM
1440	ETON COLLEGE FOUNDED	
1455	FIRST BOOK PRINTED – GUTENBURG BIBLE	
1463/1475	MUSTANSIR BILLAH	32ND. IMAM
1430/1520	SYED IMAM SHAH SON OF PIR HASSAN KABIRDIN	
1452/1519	LEONARDO DA VINCI ERA	LAST SUPPER-1495
1492	CHRISTOPHER COLUMBUS DISCOVERS THE W.INDIES INTRODUCES TOBACCO TO EUROPE	
1474/1493	ABDUS SALAAM	33RD. IMAM
1480	SPANISH INQUISITION	
1494	TREATY OF TORDESILLAS – SPAIN AND PORTUGAL DIVIDE THE KNOWN WORLD BETWEEN THEM	
1493/1496	GHARIB MIRZA	34TH. IMAM
1497	**VASCO DA GAMA FIRST LANDS IN MOMBASA**	
1496/1509	ABUZAR ALI	35TH. IMAM
1503/1566	NOSTRADAMUS	
1504	LEONARDO DA VINCI PAINTS MONA LISA	

1509/1514	MURAD MIRZA	36TH. IMAM
1509	KING HENRY VIII ON ENGLISH THRONE	
1514/1516	ZULFIQAR ALI	37TH. IMAM
1516/1550	NURUDDIN ALI	38TH. IMAM
1532	ANGLICAN CHURCH CREATED BY HENRY VIII	
1538	HENRY VIII ISSUES ENGLISH BIBLE	
1538	HENRY VIII BUILDS PALACE ON THE GROUNDS OF OATLANDS PARK FOR HIS 4TH. WIFE ANNE OF CLEAVES	
1542/1605	HUMAYUN AND AKBAR – MOGUL RULERS OF INDIA	
1550/1585	KHALLILULLAH ALI	39TH. IMAM
1558	ELIZABETH I BECOMES QUEEN OF ENGLAND	
1562	START OF AFRICAN SLAVE TRADE	
1582	POPE GREGORY XIII INTRODUCES GREGORIAN CALENDAR (England and English possessions adopt Gregorian Calendar in 1752.)	
1585/1628	NIZAR II	40TH. IMAM
1585/1616	SHAKESPEARE	
1594	PORTUGUESE BUILD FORT JESUS IN MOMBASA	
1604	FIRST ENGLISH DICTIONARY – A TABLE ALPHABETICAL BY ROBERT CAUDREY	

1606/1669	REMBRANDT	
1607	ENGLISH COLONY OF JAMESTOWN ESTABLISHED IN VIRGINIA	
1608	GALILEO	
622	FIRST ENGLISH NEWSPAPER – WEEKLY NEWS	
1642	ISSAC NEWTON AT CAMBRIDGE UNIVERSITY	
1628/1660	SAYED ALI	41ST. IMAM
1660	HON.EAST INDIA COMPANY FOUNDED BY BRITISH	
1662	TEA INTRODUCED TO BRITAIN	
1660/1694	HASAN ALI BAKAR SHAH	42ND. IMAM
1666	TAJ MAHAL BUILT BY SHAH JEHAN	
1694/1730	KASSIM ALI	43RD. IMAM
1707	ENGLAND/SCOTLAND UNION TO BECOME GREAT BRITAIN	
1717	FIRST MASONIC LODGE IN LONDON	
1729	SULTANS OF OMAN TAKE CONTROL OF EAST AFRICAN COAST, INCLUDING KENYA	
1729	PUTNEY BRIDGE OPENED IN LONDON	
1730/1792	ABUL HASSANALI SHAH	44TH. IMAM
1732/1799	GEORGE WASHINGTON FIRST U.S.PRESIDENT	
1770	CAPTAIN COOK CLAIMS	

AUSTRALIA FOR BRITISH

| 1770/1827 | BEETHOVEN | |
| 1776 | AMERICAN DECLARATION OF INDEPENDENCE | |

1784   FIRST GOLF CLUB, ST.ANDREWS, SCOTLAND

1784   BENJAMIN FRANKLIN

1789   FRENCH REVOLUTION

1790   DUKE OF YORK, SON OF GEORGE III
MOVES INTO OATLANDS PALACE

1792/1817   KHALILLULAH ALI   45TH. MAM

1798   NELSON VICTORY – BATTLE OF
THE NILE

1785/1866   IMAM BEGUM –KUTCH/KARACHI/
BOMBAY

1803   1ST.PUBLIC RAIL STATION
WANDSWORTH TO CROYDON

1807   ABOLITION OF SLAVERY IN
ENGLAND

1809/1882   CHARLES DARWIN

1812/1870   CHARLES DICKENS

1815   NAPOLEON DEFEAT AT WATERLOO

1817/1881   HASAN ALI SHAH   46TH.IMAM
AGA KAHN I, IRAN/SINDH

1818/1883   KARL MARX

1829   FIRST.OXFORD CAMBRIDGE BOAT RACE
FROM PUTNEY BRIDGE

1829	GEORGE STEVENSON & STEAM ENGINE
1832	HOUSE OF COMMONS EMPOWERED IN BRITAIN
1837/1901	QUEEN VICTORIA QUEEN OF ENGLAND AND EMPRESS OF INDIA
1838	FIRST JAMAT KHANA IN ZANZIBAR
1840/1926	MONET
1841	CITY OF HONG KONG FOUNDED BY BRITISH
1842	BRITISH TROOPS MASSACRED IN KHYBER PASS
1851	1ST.BATCH OF EIGHT INDIAN DOCTORS GRADUATE FROM GRANT MEDICAL COLLEGE IN BOMBAY
1855	ELPHINSTON COLLEGE BOMBAY STARTS SCHOOL OF LAW
1855	LIVINGSTONE DISCOVERS THE VICTORIA FALLS
1856	**OATLANDS PALACE BECOMES OATLANDS PARK HOTEL WEYBRIDGE, FIRST MANAGER MR. PEPPERCORN**
1857	ELGAR
	BOMBAY UNIVERSITY COMES INTO BEING
	INDIAN SEPOY MUTINY
	BAHADUR SHAH ZAFAR, LAST MOGHUL EMPEROR OF INDIA DEPOSED BY BRITISH AND EXILED IN BURMA ENGLISH REPLACES URDU AS COURT LANGUAGE

OF INDIA

1859	DARWIN PUBLISHES ORIGIN OF SPECIES
1859	**FIRST OIL WELL DUG IN TITUSVILLE, PENNSYLVANIA USA**
1860	ABRAHAM LINCOLN ELECTED PRESIDENT OF U.S.
1863	START OF LONDON UNDERGROUND
1867	DOMINION OF CANADA FOUNDED
1869	OPENING OF SUEZ CANAL
1876	ALEXANDER GRAHAM BELL FIRST TELEPHONE
1877	FIRST EVER CRICKET TEST BETWEEN ENGLAND AND AUSTRALIA PLAYED AT THE MELBOURNE CRICKETGROUND
1880/1972	COUNT HASHAM JAMAL
1881/1885	AGA ALI SHAH 47TH.IMAM AGA KHAN II
1881/1973	PICASSO
1885	INDIAN NATIONAL CONGRESS FORMED IN INDIA
1885/1957	SULTAN MOHAMED SHAH 48TH.IMAM, AGA KHAN III, BORN KARACHI
1886	BRITAIN/GERMANY CARVE UP E.AFRICA INTO KENYA, UGANDA, GERMAN TANGANYKA AND ARAB COASTAL STRIP
1887	BRITAIN LEASES COASTAL STRIP FROM SULTAN OF ZANZIBAR
1888	**FIRST JAMAT KHANA IN MOMBASA**

WITH MUKHI SULEMAN VERJEE

1890	BRITISH INFLUENCE IN KENYA BEGINS
1895	**JANMOHAMED HASHAM VERJEE FAMILY COMMENCES MIGRATION FROM INDIA TO AFRICA**
1895	OSCAR WILDE
1896	RAILWAY LINE FROM MOMBASA REACHES KISUMU IN 1901 AND KAMPALA IN 1931
1901	COMMONWEALTH OF AUSTRALIA COMES INTO EXISTENCE
1903	WRIGHT BROTHERS FLY FOR THE FIRST TIME
1905	KASSAM JANMOHAMED BORN IN MOMBASA
1905	1ST ROTARY CLUB FOUNDED IN CHICAGO BY PAUL HARRIS
1908	BOY SCOUTS MOVEMENT STARTED BY BADEN POWELL
1908	**OIL DISCOVERED IN PERSIA**
1910	UNION OF SOUTH AFRICA COMES INTO BEING
1911	ALIGARH ACHIEVES UNIVERSITY STATUS
1912	TITANIC SINKS ON MAIDEN VOYAGE
1914	PANAMA CANAL OPENS
1914/1918	FIRST WORLD WAR
1916	OATLANDS PARK HOTEL

REQUISITIONED AS CASUALTY HOSPITAL
FOR NEW ZEALAND FORCES SERVING IN
FRANCE, NEW ZEALAND AVENUE
NAMED IN THEIR MEMORY

1917   RUSSIAN REVOLUTION -
            LENIN COMES TO POWER

**1918   AGA KHAN EDUCATION BOARD
            APPOINTED AND FIRST AGA KHAN
            SCHOOL OPENED IN MOMBASA. VERJEE
            BOYS GO OVERSEAS FOR FURTHER
            EDUCATION**

1920   KENYA BECOMES A BRITISH
            CROWN COLONY

            NEW JAMAT KHANA IN NAIROBI

            LEAGUE OF NATIONS FORMED –
            SULTAN MOHAMED
            SHAH ONE OF EARLY PRESIDENTS

1925   HITLER PUBLISHES MEIN KAMPF

1925/1927   JANMOHAMED HASHAM MUKHI
            OF MOMBASA JAMATKHANA

1926   BIRTH OF SISTER MALEK - SULTAN
            DIED FOLLOWING YEAR

1927   OIL DISCOVERED IN IRAQ

1928   BIRTH OF SISTER ROSHAN

1929   BIRTH OF SISTER SULTAN

1928/1931   JANMOHAMED HASHAM PRESIDENT
            OF MOMBASA COUNCIL

**1931   REGAL CINEMA BUILDING
            COMPLETION**

AMEER JANMOHAMED BORN IN
KISUMU 6TH JUNE
JANMOHAMED HASHAM DIED IN
MOMBASA 18TH JUNE

FIRST **NYALI BRIDGE OPENED
CONNECTING MOMBASA ISLAND TO
MAINLAND NORTH**

**IMPERIAL AIRWAYS START SERVICE
BETWEEN LONDON/NAIROBI**

1936	SULTAN MOHAMED SHAH APPOINTS KASSAM JANMOHAMED AS MUKHI AND BKS VERJEE AS KAMADIA OF LONDON JAMAT 10 TH APRIL 1936
1936	GOLDEN JUBILEE OF SULTAN MOHAMED SHAH
1938	**OIL DISCOVERED IN SAUDI ARABIA**
1939/1945	**SECOND WORLD WAR**
1941	PEARL HARBOUR
1945	AMERICANS DROP ATOMIC BOMBS ON HIROSHIMAAND NAGASAKI
1946	DIAMOND JUBILEE OF SULTAN MOHAMED SHAH
1947	**INDIAN INDEPENDENCE AND END OF 200 YEARS OF BRITISH RAJ CREATION OF PAKISTAN AFTER PARTITION**
1948	STATE OF ISRAEL COMES INTO BEING
1950	KASSAM JANMOHAMED DIES AT AGE OF 45
	NAIROBI RECEIVES ROYAL CHARTER AS CITY

1951	HABIB KESHAVJEE FAMILY LEAVE SOUTH AFRICA TO SETTLE IN KENYA
1952/1972	BADRUDIN'S SPORT HOUSE ERA
1952	MAU MAU UPRISING IN KENYA
1954	BIRTH OF EL-QUASSIM IN MOMBASA
1956	**AKJ JOINS MOMBASA ROTARY CLUB**
1957	**SHAH KARIM AL-HUSSAYNI 49TH.IMAM AGA KHAN IV**
	GHANA, FIRST SUB-SAHARAN COUNTRY BECOMES INDEPENDENT
1963	**KENYAN INDEPENDENCE**
	PRESIDENT KENNEDY ASSASSINATION
1962/1964	AKJ KAMADIA MOMBASA CHIEF AMAT KHANA
1964/1966	AKJ MUKHI MOMBASA CHIEF JAMAT KHANA
1965/1966	AKJ PRESIDENT MOMBASA ROTARY CLUB
1968/1971	AKJ PRESIDENT MOMBASA PROVINCIAL COUNCIL
1969/1970	AKJ DISTRICT GOVERNOR R. INTERNATIONAL DISTRICT 220
1967	CHICAGO HAS FIRST JAMAT KHANA IN US
1971	E-MAIL ERA BEGINS
1972	**AKJ MOVES TO LONDON**

1973/1978	WHITEMAN'S DAIRY ERA
1979/1982	UFTONRIDGE/WOLVERBURGH ERA
1981/1982	AKJ PRESIDENT KENSINGTON ROTARY CLUB
1982	IMRAN BORN IN LONDON
1982	SWISS COTTAGE ERA
1986	OATLANDS PARK HOTEL ERA
1987	SALIM BORN IN TORONTO
1999	MA AND ROSHAN PASSED AWAY
2001	9/11
2003	FIRST AGA KHAN ACADEMY INAUGURATED IN MOMBASA
2007/2008	GOLDEN JUBILEE OF IMAMAT OF SHAH KARIM AL HUSSAYNI AGA KHAN

INDEX